White Elephants

ON YARD SALES, RELATIONSHIPS, AND FINDING WHAT WAS MISSING

KATIE HAEGELE

MICROCOSM PUBLISHING
2012

White Elephants
ON YARD SALES, RELATIONSHIPS, AND
FINDING WHAT WAS MISSING

Katie Haegele

Released June 1, 2012
First printing
ISBN 978-1-934620-28-1
This is Microcosm #76105

Illustrated by Helen Entwisle
Fonts by Ian Lynam
Edited by Joe Biel and Adam Gnade
Designed by Joe Biel

Distributed by IPG and Turnaround, UK

Microcosm Publishing
112C S. Main St.
Lansing, KS 66043-1501
&
636 SE 11th Ave.
Portland, OR 97214
www.microcosmpublishing.com

Mother's Day —
2017

Dear Mom,
Thank you for:
- Garage Sales
- Yard Sales
- Estate Sales
- Drives in the country
- Spontaneous Stops
- Your always beautiful, cozy home.

- Our elusive hunt for the taxidermied snowy owl.

I love You!
Always,
Eldest

Contents

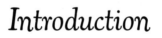

Introduction

I GREW UP IN AN OLD TOWN THAT LIES RIGHT ON the city limit of Philadelphia. I live here still. In fact I live around the corner and up the street from the house I grew up in, which is where my mother still lives. She and I talk every day and see each other almost as often, and I'd like to say that I probably wouldn't live here, and we probably wouldn't be as close as we are, if my father hadn't died 12 years ago when I was 21. I'd like to say this because I think it must be true, but I try not to think about what-ifs where his life is concerned. They don't make any difference; they don't even make sense. That was what happened, not something different, and here I am, standing in the middle of my life.

And good things have come out of the sadness, as they always do. Making friends with my mom has been one of the good things. We always got along okay, but we only got close after my dad died and I was living at home again with her, just the two of us. A few days after his funeral I left the apartment I'd shared with a friend and limped back home, me and the narrow-bodied cat I'd adopted that spring. I stayed there for five years. It wasn't always easy, for me or for Mom. Sometimes I came home late, fumbling at the front door, drunk, waking her up and annoying her. Other times I annoyed her by leaving every mug in my messy bedroom, half-filled with cold milky tea, teetering all around the room. But there were many nights we sat in the living room, ignoring the TV and talking all evening. On Halloween, if the weather was mild, we'd sit on the porch to give out candy, whispering about all our neighbors. Once a week we had dinner at this pubby restaurant we used to like, before it turned into a sports bar. I'd have a beer and Mom would have a glass of white wine, and we'd tease the waiter by calling him "The Genius" because he always remembered our drink order, which was always the same.

This rummaging pastime, though, this was something I had to work at. Rooting through other people's old stuff has been one of my favorite things to do since I was in high school, but not my mom's. She didn't get it. When I was 15 and having a best-friend love-affair with Laura R., she and I used to go to the Salvation Army and bring back wonderful clothes—t-shirts with goofy ads for local businesses, tight seventies leather jackets in weird colors, and one time, an amazing chintzy black polyester waitress uniform, the kind that's all one piece and has white collars and cuffs. Back then, my mother made me put that stuff through the laundry separate from everything else, she was so skeeved out by it. But once I was living there again as a grownup I guess she decided to get over it. One Saturday I talked her into doing the yard sale circuit with me and she didn't seem to hate it, so I kept circling the ads in the classifieds every week, hoping she'd want to go again. I didn't have a driver's license—still don't—so I knew if I could get Mom into the rummaging game we could go all over the place, and we did. Still do.

Every Wednesday the local newspaper would come and we'd go through the classifieds looking for yard sales. Over time we've learned to assess a listing's potential with real accuracy. If it says NO EARLY BIRDS it will probably have cheesy stuff we don't want, like Beanie Babies and other dubious collectibles. Things called "estate sales" are more promising but they're often overpriced. There was one address we kept seeing in the classifieds and eventually came to recognize as the home of an antiques dealer. Technically it was a yard sale—for sure, it was held right there in the lady's weedy little yard. But looking through her stuff felt more like visiting an antiques store. She had boxes of hundred-year-old postcards, terrifying farm tools, dressmaker's dummies, things like that. I love those too, but not at a yard sale. People of the neighborhood, give me your scuffed jewelry, your chipped serving bowls, your *National Geographics*! I want to do the digging for my buried treasures, not have it done for me.

When I moved away from home for the second time, it was into an apartment in a pretty little brick building around the corner, the one I used to walk past every day on my way to school. Mom and I kept our Saturday rummage date, and at some point it occurred to me that recording these yard sale moments might be fun or funny or even worthwhile. I was deeply into making zines by that point and the obsessive format seemed perfect for a project like this. Sure enough, I made that first issue of *White Elephants* and have done so every summer since. It's become an important part of the yard sale process: Sit on my couch and circle the likely-looking ads, drinking my coffee and waiting for Mom to come pick me up. Look out the window of the passenger side of her car, watching the suburbs slide past. Paw through other people's old junk like I'm looking for something, because let's be honest, I am. Come home and write up a report, like a private eye.

At this point most of the stuff I own used to belong to somebody else. I've bought hand towels with owls on them, a wicker basket shaped like a chicken, and a yellow wire sculpture of a chicken with its middle hollowed out like a basket, which must have some intended use but I don't know what it is. One morning, on a card table on a lady's front lawn, I found an ugly decorative plate with too many flowers on it that says, in curlicue cursive, NEVER UNDERESTIMATE THE POWER OF A WOMAN, and now it hangs on the wall over my kitchen sink. I won't even tell you about the actual trash I've salvaged, the family photographs and driving school certificates I've picked out of people's garbage cans or the slightly more useful furniture and books I've found, discarded, on the curb. I will say that I love all the things I've found, completely and without irony. Well, the "Power of a Woman" plate is about fifty-percent ironic, I guess. But I'm not sure if ironic is the right word. It sounds so calculated, and kind of mean-spirited. The feeling I get from kitsch is more touching than that, more sad. A thing becomes kitschy once it is no longer fabulous, but is haunted by the ghost of its former fabulousness. That's how kitsch works. It's going but it's not gone yet.

A few years ago this girl I know through doing zines told me she was planning to start a distro and call it Saudade. I wished her luck and asked her: What does the name mean? She told me it's a Portuguese word that doesn't translate too neatly into English, but that it means nostalgia, kind of, a sense of longing for something that is lost and probably can't be found again. Well hey, I thought. I know that feeling. By coincidence that same week I was in one of the small libraries in my neighborhood, looking for something to read, when I found a book about the city of Trieste by the Welsh travel writer Jan Morris. I sat on the floor to look through it a bit, even though I'd never heard of Trieste and didn't know where it was. (It's in Italy.) Right on the second page the writer mentioned a word of Welsh Gaelic: hiraeth. It means a kind of nostalgic sadness, though supposedly it too has no translation into English. As far as I can tell it means homesickness but for an idealized home, someplace that never existed but in a perfect world would materialize and welcome you to it. It would be neat, tidy I mean, to say that I've been looking for a sense of home ever since I lost my dad, and that might be a part of it, but it's not the whole story. The feeling that nudges me toward these secondhand things is something that's been with me for a long time.

He was nostalgic too though, my dad. Sentimental, even. It was not a quality of his I always admired. He could be sappy, tearing up over a movie even though day-to-day, when it came to the real stuff, he was often bristly, unpredictable, even mean. But there were ways in which his romantic sense of himself was deeply appealing. It was this way he had of creating himself, of being an artist not in his work but with his life, and it has had a big impact on me.

He liked and understood beautiful things long before he could afford them. You could fairly describe him as elegant. Better yet, snazzy, with a winking, knowing kind of glamour. He grew up in a working class neighborhood in Philadelphia, in a narrow rowhouse with a stoop out front and a tiny yard in back. Roxborough wasn't as rough as some other parts of Philly but it was the kind of neighborhood, as he liked to say, where you wouldn't have to go too far out of your way to get into a brick fight. Nonetheless, you are who you are. I really believe that. When he was a kid, whenever they went to the library, he'd look up *Vogue* magazine and sit there looking at the beautiful pictures of the beautiful clothes. His sense of himself in the world was something nobody gave him. It was all his own.

He should have been named John or Michael or something like that but they named him Monroe—some confusing story about a family friend who'd agreed to pay for a college education if they named their third son after him, which he didn't do. My dad was saddled with this unusual name that embarrassed him his whole life, but even still, he owned it. Monroe Jay. He could be theatrical and silly, confident at restaurants and charming with women. He wore cufflinks when they weren't in style. On the rare occasions that he'd smoke one of my mom's cigarettes he'd stand in the kitchen and do impressions with them, like his imitation of "a German mathematician," for which he pinched the cigarette between his thumb and forefinger and took short little puffs with a pissy expression on his face. A lot of times I had no idea what he was talking about but he treated me like I did. Or maybe he thought I actually did. He gave me *My Antonia* to read when I was 11, took me to a jazz club downtown when I was 19. One day, when I was just about to blossom into a baby teenager, he walked past the mirror above the coat rack where I was brushing my hair and told me, with an admiration I could tell was real, that I looked like Veronica Lake. *Who?*

The day after he died I walked upstairs like a zombie and took the one thing of his I knew I needed, a framed poster from the Charlie Chaplin movie *Gold Rush* in German: *Gold Rausch*. In it a figure of Charlie Chaplin is painted in black, his body in two halves with the leg-half cocked sideways to exaggerate his heel-clicking stance. The picture is stylish and sad, funny and odd, and in some way that I couldn't articulate to myself at the time it represented my dad to me. It was my dad. That movie was made twenty years before he was born, but it seemed somehow to be an extension of him, something he thought into existence.

When he died his goneness felt abrupt, and sometimes in my memory that's how it was—here one minute, vanished the next. But in fact he was sick for several years, not exactly fading all that time, but changing, preparing. He was diagnosed with lymphatic cancer during my first year of college, and when I came home for the summer he told me. "Does that mean you're gonna die? Like, soon?" We were outside the ice cream place we went to sometimes, where he'd kind of awkwardly asked me to go that night, just the two of us. "I don't know," he said plainly. Then he nodded. "Probably, yeah." Over the next four years he tried to figure things out, and he picked up some new-agey habits that were kind of obnoxious, like meditating and acting sanctimonious about it. But his old black humor remained intact. At one point, when he was getting sicker and suffering through chemo but still felt strong enough to go into work, he bought a big animatronic crow for his office that scream-talked when you pushed a button. "Raaah! The end is near! Raaaaaaaaaw!" He was going but he wasn't gone yet.

Nostalgia is a kind of maligned concept, but when I talk about it I mean something existential—not a retro diner with doo-wop on the jukebox or old people talking about how much better things used to be, but the sad longing of hiraeth and saudade, the loneliness and melancholy that run underneath everything in life, the feelings that are always there, humming like power lines. I think it's something we all carry around with us, even if some of us seem to feel it more intensely than others. Maybe you deal with your saudade, when it rises up, by listening to a certain song or going for a long drive. I address mine in the basements of old churches, handling jewelry and dresses and little figurines that someone else once saw and bought, and used and loved. These things vibrate with the lives they've been a part of, and I fill my home with them because I like the company.

I never got to have an adult relationship with my father, so I didn't get to ask him what Charlie Chaplin meant to him, or tell him what dressing up in some lady's kooky old clothes means to me. The things he and I have in common were still only nascent in me when he died. But even though I find neat conclusions annoying, I guess if I were being honest I'd admit that what I do, I do in part because it keeps me close to him. He and I were the romantic ones, the sensitive ones, and if he were still here, even if we never did get around to talking about it, I know he'd like the odd, sad, funny person I've become.

But you know, I didn't set out to make such a big deal out of all this. I really did just want to tell you about the weird shit I found on people's front lawns. I hope you'll enjoy reading about my yard sale adventures as much as I enjoyed writing about them, which was an awful lot.

Guideposts
Yard Sale Season No. 1

THE FIRST FIND OF THE SEASON WAS ONE OF THE best. The minute I saw it I loved this wicker handbag, with its metal clasp closure and yarn flowers sewn to the front. It's large, with stiff handles and a flip-top lid on hinges, just the thing for the newly warm weather. One dollar for that little prize. I also found a crazy record album by a seventies band called The Incredible String Band. I wish you could see the cover of this album. It's so insane. There are 11 people—six adults and five kids—dressed like circus clowns/ vagabonds. There's a dog too. I guess it's a hippie "family" kind of situation. I got to chatting with the lady whose house it was and told her what a kick I got out of the picture, and she showed me some of the other things she'd set out on the tables in her driveway, including a huge floppy sun hat I admired but knew I shouldn't attempt to pull off. She was a woman in her late fifties, younger than my mom by just a little. She had the look of someone who has lived it up and been sad in equal measure, and she seemed to approve of my interest in her junk. "I'm glad you care about...what went before," she said.

The other house we went to was a few blocks away from home—my apartment building and my mom's house being around the corner. These folks lived in a sweet row house on one of the small blocks near the center of town. I love row houses. They look so cozy and safe tucked in next to each other. They feel cozy inside, too.

This event appeared to be an estate sale, which is touchy. They often have interesting things rather than junk, but depending on who's hosting them they can be weird and sad. The family of a freshly dead person feels bad, usually, but somehow it feels worse when an estate professional handles things, since they hawk the stuff in an impersonal way. It reminds me of funerals I've been to where the priest says nice things about the person who's died but clearly never knew them. Mom and I walked timidly up the stairs and right inside the front door saw a beautiful old bird cage, which encouraged me to go all the way in. A woman was standing near the doorway, though she was trying to act like she hadn't noticed we were coming in. The room was dark even though it was the middle of the day. I admired a pretty old sewing box and the notions inside it, which the woman told me had been her mother's, but I didn't buy anything. The air in that room was heavy and I felt awkward and sorry and wanted to leave. A middle-aged man—maybe the lady's brother—was out front furiously yanking around a garden hose. When Mom and I walked past we said hello but he didn't respond. My guess is his sister wanted to sell some of their mother's stuff and he didn't want her to, but it's impossible to say what was really happening. You never know what goes on with families.

Back at home I was excited to have new music to play on my record player, but I remembered that I'd been having all this trouble getting both speakers to play at once. I called Mom and between her and my mechanically-minded sister they were able to fiddle with the wires until the sound was even. Liz even fixed the mechanism on the player's arm, which had come loose and made the needle skitter across a record when I tried to lift it up. I was delighted to have the afternoon to play records, but this new one was terrible, I have to say. Endless hippie jammy jams. Bleh. I've held onto the album though. It's awesome to look at, a good artifact to add to my museum.

Rummage sales are better than yard sales, mom and I have decided. I had dinner at her house on Wednesday, the day the paper is delivered, and I waited until after we ate to sit in "my" armchair and go through the classifieds. Score. There were two church rummage sales that weekend and two the following, all of them at Protestant churches within a mile or two of home I've passed a million times on foot or in the car or on the bus but, until we started making a project out of rummage sales, never had occasion to go inside. That's part of the pleasure of all this—the snooping. Accidentally walking down wrong hallways into a preschool classroom, quiet and still as a summer day. Church halls and basements feel a lot like people's homes, I find. They're full of personal artifacts, like drawings by the Sunday school kids and bulletin boards covered in snapshots.

"Mom, where's Mount Holly Methodist?" I asked her. She was tucked into her usual spot on the couch, poking away at a large cross-stitch picture of an amaryllis flower in a vase.

"On Mount Holly Avenue," she said in her deadpan way, which could have a question buried at the center of it— *why don't you ever remember where anything is?*—but then again it might not have.

The sale started Thursday evening and continued the following morning, and since my mom never wants to go anywhere once it's dark out we planned to go on Friday. I work from home so I can do things like this, especially when I don't have much writing work coming in, which happens often enough.

Mom picked me up in her car and we drove to the imposing old stone church. The sale held in this seemingly sleepy place turned out to be the site of two acrimonious disputes. Although, on the sleepy tip, there was actually an old man asleep by the door in a folding chair.

I don't know what was going on with me, but I wasn't in top form that day. I walked in and right away started looking through a pile of purses when this woman I recognized from other rummage sales—there's a crew of us— picked up an adorable pink-and-purple-plaid Bermuda bag right from under my nose that I hadn't even noticed there. She's a woman not much older than me, which makes her younger than the average person on the sale circuit.

"That's really cute," I said, my heart turning black.

"I know! It reminds me of my preppy days!" She pretended to sound lighthearted about it but she clutched that clutch with a death grip. She didn't want me getting it and I don't blame her.

Do you know what a Bermuda bag is, by the way? I had not heard that term before but that's what my mom called it when I told her my sad story. It's a kind of oval-shaped fabric bag with a wooden or plastic handle where the fabric part is detachable. The idea is that you can change your bag to match your outfit, which is ridiculous and outdated but sweet and pretty clever, too.

The other bad moment I had at this sale took place between me and Mom, when she found this set of small decorative plates with birds on them that I would have loved to have had in my apartment. When I said so, she offered me one. I just shook my head in dismay. Mom, don't you know the fun of rummage sales is in the *finding*? I did not find these, therefore I remain disappointed. All I ended up getting that day was a wind-up E.T. that walks toward you on its plastic feet like a robot, and a big button that says "I've got it!" So-so finds, but you can't hit the jackpot every time.

The next morning we drove over to mom's old neighborhood to go to a sale at an Episcopal church called St. Barnabas. This is an original suburb. It was a development plotted out before the suburbs existed as such—during the 1940s. It was built on the vast flat moonlike emptiness of leveled ground because they tore all the trees out. It doesn't look like a moonscape now because the trees and shrubs planted by new homeowners 60 years ago have reached their full height and they fill the empty spaces, decorating the neighborhood like flowering furniture. The identical houses aren't identical anymore either. Now they have different shapes with additions and decks and new roofs. It's still very quiet over here, though, and a bit of a time warp. There are no sidewalks and the streets are wide and paved with blacktop that seems perfectly smooth, so your car rolls quietly along. Nothing else around here is like that, not in Philadelphia, city of potholes and everything busted.

There's something touching about St. Barnabas, the way it's right in the middle of a suburban neighborhood, on a plot between two houses and not much bigger than either of them. It reminds me of how our family dog, who had no dog friends, used to mince around with the two cats, trying to look dainty like them.

This sale turned out to be interesting. It was a classic "jumble," with a number of wooden tables all heaped with clothing and other junk. But the building is newer than the others we've gone to, maybe it was built in the fifties, and it had the fresh feeling of a place that's used regularly, like I was in someone's living room. It made me want to be less disheveled and more polite than usual.

I scored a few excellent items, including an unopened counted cross-stitch kit that said "Beware of attack cat." It came with a flat wooden black cat figure to glue onto the finished piece. I pictured Trixie, my companion cat who is herself black, doing her tap dance of excited play-fighting back at home, as she could surely vibe the awesomeness of this find. I know Mom was in the market for baskets and vases that she could use to make flower arrangements for the garden club we both belong to (but for which I'm too lazy to ever contribute arrangements), but I don't know if she found any. I wasn't paying attention, and I got unnerved by an encounter with St. Barnabas' lady pastor. I was carrying around the cat cross-stitch and probably smiling about it because a plain-dressed woman with a large cross around her neck came up to me with the intention of starting a conversation. She wasn't your usual rummage sale kook, she was greeting me from a position of authority, and she seemed to be around my age, no older than her mid-30s. This freaked me out for some reason.

"Looks like you found something good there," she said in a fond, teasing way.

"Oh! Yeah, totally. I enjoy these kinds of embroidery projects. It's soothing." There, I said too much, soothing means I have problems and now she knows it. We stood facing each other with awkward smiles and then I ducked my head and turned away to examine a colander on the table next to me.

"I think that lady is the pastor!" I hissed to Mom when I found her a few minutes later.

"Well yes, I think she might be, Katie," said my mom in her voice that means What is the big deal?

Whatever, I also found a neat magnetic memo board thing that seems to have been intended for use in a kindergarten classroom or something because it has the alphabet printed in bright red along the top. What's weird about it—and there is usually something weird—is that some letters are repeated, some three times, some only two, so as I read it I felt vaguely dizzy and worried that I was about to get one my headaches. It looks like this:

ABBCDEEEFFGGHIII

And so on. It's trippy but useful and I will happily buy it for ten cents and hang it in my kitchen, thank you, where I can tack up shopping lists and cleaning schedules. I found a fake gold chain and a fake gold pendant with a cluster of flowers painted white over the metal, which I feel looks downtown in a rich, Lucky magazine kind of way. I made the best find on the way out, where they had books and cards on a bookcase in the hallway—an unused box of stationery from the seventies, green paper with a photo image of daisies and grass running up one side, with matching green envelopes. I love writing letters and at this point I have probably 12 or so regular pen-pals—people I met through zines. Whenever I find it I snap up writing paper, ugly or pretty or both.

Later, at home, I put on a record and sat down to write a couple of letters I'd owed for a while. I used some notecards though, not the new stationery set; it's too new. It needs to do its time in the drawer first.

Some days I just feel like hearing a record, which is a different experience than listening to the radio or my iPod, in part because the music I have on vinyl is old stuff that I don't listen to any other way. I bought the record player one day several years ago in a kind of panic. In the months after my father died my mom gave and threw away his things with abandon. She couldn't get rid of them fast enough. I was living back at home with her at the time, and one morning on my way out the door to my stupid job at a low-rent business magazine I saw all my dad's records stacked up on either side of the front door.

"What are you doing? You can't get rid of these!" I told her, freaking out, but she could, and she intended to. As a kid I'd started to develop my own taste in music by finding these records, fondling the brittle paper inside and studying the liner notes and pictures, then listening to them on my parents' nice stereo without their permission, wearing huge headphones so they wouldn't hear and know what I was doing. The Stones, the Beatles, the Band, Joe Cocker, some jazz, lots of soul music, and several operas: Music was important to my dad and there are some songs that still make me think of him and nothing else, like the costumey sadness of Kurt Weill. God he would have loved Alan Cumming and Cyndi Lauper in The Threepenny Opera. At least I think he would have approved. I wish I could ask him.

Anyway, the thought of losing these records made me go cold with something like real fear, but the hoarding of objects is one area where my mother is perfectly unsympathetic to my feelings. She told me if I wanted to keep any of them I'd better take care of it now because this afternoon the "guys" were coming, some men she'd hired to haul away the old things that I guess they will either use themselves or sell, so in several awkward trips up the stairs I carried heavy armloads of them to my childhood bedroom, cursing that I was already late for work and trying not to cry. I'm glad to have something to listen to them on but honestly, I only bought the player because she made me feel that keeping records I couldn't listen to was something only a crazy person would do.

So, before I sat down to write my letters I put on some Otis Redding. One of Dad's all-time favorites and now one of mine. Did you know he was only 26 years old when he died, Otis Redding? His voice and his lyrics were so husky and worldly, it's hard to remember he was so young. But back then people were grown up by that age. I think in the old days everybody actually wanted to be an adult, whereas now everybody wants to stay a kid.

I like to write letters at my desk, which is an ugly one with a fake wood top and metal filing drawers, just like you'd have in a real office. I bought it new from an office supplier to make a kind of joke to myself, a comment on the idea of "real" jobs versus "real" work, since I use the desk to do my writing. It sits beside a window in my living room that overlooks a huge horse chestnut tree. The tree is magnificent this time of year, all its tiny new leaves glowing a pastel green when the sun catches them right. I did some writing but mostly I just sat there at the desk, quiet for a while, the Otis Redding making it feel like church.

•　　•　　•

Mom and I went to so many other sales this month it made our heads spin. I'm just gonna bang them out for you, one after the other.

St. Martin's Lutheran

This church hall had a stage, like the one from the hall in the parish I grew up in, and the stage was where they had arranged cafeteria tables full of books. I got *Best American Poetry, 1997*, which seemed important because 1997 was a year I was completely uninterested in poetry so I had some catching up to do. Many of these poems turned out to be dated in style and not, in my estimation, very memorable or exciting, sort of dead on the page. But a few had arresting images, which is usually all I ask of a poem. There's a good one by Charles Simic where he talks about seeing something moving in the street late at night while he's standing on his porch. I also snagged an awesome wide yellow plastic wicker-looking belt, and had a nice conversation with an eccentric old woman, so tiny next to me, in the check-out line that ended at a stainless steel table in the church kitchen where two women sat at cash registers. The woman had found a mug with a kitten on it to give to her friend, who loves all animals.

Swedenborg Library Sale

Oh, the New Church Swedenborg. This place is a church and college that are legendary around here, though no one seems to know exactly what it is. They have green grounds like a golf course, magnificent gardens, and a massive white cathedral with spires and everything, sitting there like it was dropped down from the sky. I've been looking at it my whole life and mystified by it, like, suddenly we're in the South of France? What happened? Mom and I knew nothing about this place, so we were excited to find their library sale listed in the paper this week. That allowed for a little snooping.

The college's library was across the street from the cathedral and in a much more unassuming building. I tried sizing everybody up. Were they nerdy, socially-weird kids going to a Christian college? Didn't seem to be. Everyone looked intelligent and wholesome, like they get up early every morning. At the reference desk we got directions to the sale room from an older guy with suspenders and a British accent. We made our way down a few hallways with that hard industrial carpeting that libraries always have, the brown tight-knit kind that's as hard as the linoleum underneath and gives it a little bounce. You know the kind I mean.

I like a good library sale, I have to say. It's fun to own books that are stamped with library information, and sometimes ones from smaller collections—like this one, it turned out—have a nice official bookplate pasted onto the inside cover. Mom, a lifelong big reader, disappeared into the novels, and I went over to the nonfiction books to see what I could desecrate for my zines and other "art." I like finding any kind of book that deals with women's health concerns, family relationships, or fashion, as long as it is at least 20 years old. Lately I've been getting a kick out of old cookbooks too, with their garish ghastly pictures of Jello-oriented food. I didn't see anything like this but I must have spent half an hour paging through all the art books and a huge coffee table book of photographs of the National Parks. I didn't want any of those though. I won't read them and they're too nice to destroy.

However, the religion section was full of interesting stuff, and with all the theology textbooks and prayer books it turned out to be a good way to get an introduction to this religion. It was by attempting to do this that I made an exciting discovery. On the table were several copies, in different editions and with different covers, of a book called *My Religion* by Helen Keller, the various retellings of whose life story I have always loved reading. It's the story of her childhood and the way she learns language that you get from those books. I knew she went on to have a significant and public life after she grew up but I never knew much else about it. But now I know that this was her religion!

The Swedenborgian Church is a Christian church that was started by a Swedish theologian and scientist in the 18th century. He was a mystic of sorts and he talked to angels and demons. Note to self: learn more about this. If there's one thing I like in this world it's a mystic. Note to you: This library's bookplate has a pretty line drawing of the cathedral.

I also found a great-looking Modern Library edition of *Selected Poetry of W.H. Auden*, a hardback from 1970 with a brittle blue and yellow dustcover. I sound like I'm selling this to you on eBay but honestly, it's a fantastic little book, fat but not heavy, pleasing to hold. And the poems—can't beat 'em. How about this line from "Song of the Master and Boatswain":

> "TEARS ARE ROUND, THE SEA IS DEEP;
> ROLL THEM OVERBOARD AND SLEEP."

Words to live by.

WEEPING WILLOW METHODIST

There was a starey old man lurking around but otherwise everyone was nice. They sold coffee and donuts and they'd make you a pancake or egg breakfast if you wanted one. I found a big, heavy sewing box filled with so-old-they-were-vintage sewing notions, but all I wanted was the nifty red tape measure I found inside it, so I took that out and offered the woman a quarter for it. I also found a pretty zippered case I can use for pills or makeup or something, a nice old wooden ruler, and a glass pitcher from the sixties with yellow and green flowers on it.

Mom found a stack of old issues of this religious magazine *Guideposts* that she likes. It's a funny situation with Mom. She was raised in the old-school church, with the Mass in Latin and teacher-nuns in full habits like Halloween costumes, but she drifted away from the church when she grew up, as many people her age did. She grew her hair long and married the no-religion son of a non-practicing Jew and a lapsed Catholic, but later she panicked and took me out of the public school and got me into the local parish school. Liz and I got the full treatment, confessionals and kneelers and enough symbolism to turn me into a hypersensitive poet; in my way I really took to it. But Mom struggles with it. She goes through different phases. Sometimes she goes to Mass every week and on all the arcane Holy Days of Obligation, too. Other times she'll drop back out, find she's fidgety, sitting there on the wooden pews thinking uncharitable thoughts about the people around her, and she'll need to take a few months off. She seems to find it easier to connect to the preachers on TV, the megachurch ones who have gone mainstream, and things like this magazine. I've read it and I have to say it's pretty nice. Nothing bigoted or too sanctimonious, just people's stories about overcoming hardship, like football injuries and lost pregnancies. I call it *The Tearjerker Gazette*.

Anyway. Mom gave the magazines away to an old lady who sat beside us while we sucked at hot coffee and ate a mid-morning snack. She noticed them on the table and told us she sends them to men in prison, along with other books. "You just can't send hardcovers, or anything with sharp edges," she added, leaving us to look down at our soft pretzels and muse on that unhappily for a minute.

Then my glass pitcher was arduously and messily wrapped in newspaper by a little girl who said, "Now it won't break even if it falls out of your car!"

Off to Our Lady of the Gossipy Ladies.

OUR LADY OF THE GOSSIPY LADIES
Yeah, these women weren't very nice. They tried asking personal questions about the people who live across the street from my mom, and they gave us an unkind once-over as well.

This is Mom's neighbor Joan's church though, and she's pretty nice, and I did find a nice dress. It's a long blue-green one that looked slinky on the hanger but that I somehow knew would look, on me, dowdy but charming in that young grandma way, like something a singer-songwriter from the early nineties would have worn along with some kind of floppy hat, which I decided was an okay look for a dollar, especially since I won't wear a hat like that.

The next day I belted the dress with the awesome yellow belt and wore this get-up over to my hairdresser, who'd called to tell me he had a brochure about a hair convention for me. He seemed to think I would want this information, I think, because I've told him I write for newspapers and he was hoping for some publicity. I think it's possible his son, also a hairdresser in the salon, has the hots for me, which is why I cared what I looked like. I did get a big smiley hello from him so I'll let you know what happens the next time I get my hair cut.

I also got *Time Life Great Men of Music: Mozart*, a set of four records, but it turned out to be a lot of sappy sonatas that I doubt I'll be in the mood to listen to very often. I prefer classical music that sounds like the score of a horror movie, or at least a movie with distressing domestic themes. Oh well, twenty-five cents.

A few weeks ago Mom started noticing signs appearing on a main road near us advertising a huge neighborhood-wide sale at a place called "Grey Gardens." We'd never heard of it before. Was it an apartment building? A housing development? These suburbs are too old and already built up to have a new development, and there aren't any apartments over that way. We were stumped.

So we went, and this whole neighborhood, which apparently calls itself Grey Gardens, had been transformed into a yard sale, like, street fair. One woman had even set up a striped garden tent with small tables underneath it where she served donuts and fruit and coffee. A sign on her lawn told us it was The Garden Cafe. It was so cute, I just died. Mom and I walked along the winding streets that were lined with trees in full summer bloom, kudzu climbing up and around their trunks. We walked right down the center of the street because the cars of the neighborhood seemed to know to stay off these roads. Most of the houses seemed to be participating in the sale, with small tables on their lawns or sidewalks, some of them manned by kids, which always cracks me up. We passed a few yards that were noticeably empty and quiet, and I must say I felt for those folks. Just by being busy that day or deciding not to join in, they were marked as the neighborhood grumps, and goodness knows I've been that person before.

Several sales were run by groups of families, with lots of stuff being sold at one location. On one such lawn I found an old rubber stamp making kit, a wonderful find for a zine maker. As I looked it over, images of how I would use it to make this zine formed in my mind. It came with four stampers, the painted-wooden handled kind that librarians use, each with a few metal rows for stamps. The box, an excellent bright-colored sixties thing, was still full of those tiny rubber letters you have to slide into place and then wiggle like teeth to make sure they're in there tight enough.

Another house had a big lawn we could walk around on, an easy-going lawn that wasn't clipped too short and was covered in clover. It wrapped around the back of the house and had tables and boxes all over it. We looked around for a while and Mom was about ready to give up on that sale and move on when I found a blown-up photo of a big old green Buick going down the highway, shot from behind. It was in a mat the same avocado color as the car. The man who'd taken it walked over when he saw me admiring it and told me he took it by setting the camera on the dashboard of his car while he was driving his family to California for a vacation in 1976.

"That's the year I was born!" I blurted out. In that moment it seemed like an amazing coincidence. He told me his daughter was born later that year too. When he said it he looked at me in a way I couldn't totally read—appraising, trying to see if he thought I looked the same age as his daughter, but seeing something else too, maybe himself when he was younger, back when he took the picture. It wasn't a lustful look but there was a note of that in there too somehow. Now the picture is stuck with that sticky blue gum next to the bookcase in my living room, and for as long as I have it I guess I'll remember that look on his face.

Down the street from the Buick house was a friendly couple with mild southern accents. For two dollars they sold me this fantastic hot air balloon, a decoration made of painted metal with a loop on the top for you to hang it from the ceiling. I was so taken with this thing that I put it up as soon as I got home and, after considering it for a moment, set a black cat figurine in the basket so it would look like Trixie going for a ride. The balloon hovers over my coffee table, permanently ready to lift tiny Tee up into the clouds. Mom found a pretty ceramic flower vase that's flat on one side for hanging on the wall. It has ivy painted on it and she told me she intends to put cuttings of real ivy in it. Genius.

Probably the best find, though, was a record cabinet I got for $5. It's small and seventies-green—avocado again—with two sliding doors. I can use it to store my records, which I've been accumulating since acquiring my dad's modest collection. I'm not at all interested in becoming a serious collector, but I get a lot of pleasure out of finding records at sales like these. The ones people are selling are so often the iconic, important ones, the records everybody owned, like *Mona Bone Jakon* and *Beggar's Banquet* and Fleetwood Mac's *Rumours*, and they never cost more than a quarter. It's neat to have a collection that consists only of my dad's old records and these ones I find myself, which are also old but are new to me. It's like I've managed to somehow go back in time and build a new collection there.

•   •   •

Mom has a small beach house down at the Jersey shore, in a dry town all the way at the southernmost tip of the state. Dry means it has no bars or liquor stores, and as a result most of the people who live there year-round are old and most of the people who vacation there are...well, sober. It's a pretty place, a Victorian seaside resort town that's stuck in time, even as it gets built up and overpopulated and has traffic jams like midtown Manhattan. We like it down there, especially when they do dorky community stuff, like the Fourth of July bazaar that is an excellent source of white elephants. It's held in a firehouse, which is old and quaint, and the fire trucks are blue. Such a pretty color, and it has the subtle effect of making you think no real emergencies ever happen here.

All three of us were at the shore for the Fourth, making this my sister's first rummage of the year, though it's symbolically the last one of the season. Liz doesn't live far from us, just a few miles up the road in Philly, but she doesn't really participate in the yard sale ritual. When dad died she was living close to home at college, and even though I'm the older one I moved back home and she didn't, and she's always kind of kept her distance. I'm friends with Liz too, but Mom and I have our own thing going on.

After we drank our coffee, Mom and Liz and I walked over there. The blue trucks were parked on the street to make room for the knick-knacks and hot dogs. Liz was more excited about the raffle drawing than anything else. She'd bought a ticket to win a sea kayak earlier in the season and they were to announce the winner today, just before noon.

Spread throughout the inside of the firehouse were tables of rummage stuff. These two women were selling heaps of scraps of fabric and old linens, and for twenty-five cents I got one bolt with a pattern of black and brown tree branches, which is going to get turned into a throw pillow as soon as I feel like dragging my sewing machine off its shelf and remembering how to thread the bobbin. Which might be never. I also found a great-looking wooden recipe box for 50 cents that Liz suggested I use for business cards. Clever! It smells nice on the inside. Also found a teensy old picture frame for a dime where I figured I could put the small flower cross-stitch design I'd been working on.

Then there was the book section. Lots of good things here, which is nice on a few levels—I enjoy finding good books, but I also like thinking of a community where good books are being read. There are some thrift stores near me that only have *Reader's Digest*s and it feels dismal, like there's no one in the whole neighborhood who likes to read. I found *Sewing Made Easy*, a big hardbound book with terrific fifties drawings of spools of thread and scissors decorating its powder blue endpapers, and *Fun With Crewel Embroidery* by Erica Wilson, who my mom says is the "queen" of needlework. One of her charts is for an elephant design, a white elephant, in fact, with just a simple chain-stitch outline. I took this as a good sign for the making of this zine.

When it was time for the drawing we all gathered around outside the open firehouse to listen to the names being called for different prizes, but my sister didn't win. She was listening for Elizabeth, her given name, and when the man said into the bullhorn, "The kayak goes to Aly...ssa!" Liz went, "So close!"

After everyone went to bed I sat up and finished stitching my flower. I wanted to put it in the little frame right away, and when I pulled the backing out I discovered a black-and-white photo of a woman with curled, light-colored hair and drawn-in eyebrows. It had been turned around backward, which is why I hadn't seen it before. It's printed on paper so it's just the picture that came with the frame, I guess. But it's old, from the 30s or 40s, and the woman's face looks so sweet and pretty. Now I have the photo tucked away safe in my recipe box and my flower cross-stitch in the frame, and my cat is curled up on the back of the couch as I write this, so in other words this was pretty much the best weekend ever.

I KNOW I SAID I WASN'T GONNA TALK ABOUT THE trash I've picked, but I have to tell you about this one thing. It's just too good.

All fall and winter there was some kind of major construction work being done on the basement of my old church, which is a couple blocks down from me, toward the center of town. This was mildly interesting to me since the hall in that basement was where we had our school dances. There's a little kitchen and a chapel down there too, I think. I can't remember it that well, I just remember the little vest I thought was so cool that I wore to some of the dances when I was about 12, and how much I loved a boy named Mike B. who was two years older, and how happy I was when they played Guns N' Roses.

They've been digging up huge chunks of cement from inside the building and every few days for months now a small pile of trash will appear in the parking lot, against the chain link fence. Catholic schools never ever throw anything away, so every time I took a peek I half expected the pile to be full of amazing Victorian machines, some antiques that don't have a use anymore. As long as it still works Catholic people will keep using it, however clunky and embarrassing it is. But to my surprise they seemed to be getting rid of some half-usable stuff—I saw chairs and boxes of books, things like that. I knew it was only a matter of time before I raided this trash heap, but I kept cringing away from the image in my mind of Father Devlin hearing me rustling around in there like a raccoon and pushing aside a curtain in the rectory, peering out at me and seeing straight into my puny little soul.

One night in October, before it got too cold, I walked past the church to check my mailbox at the post office. They never lock the lobby where the mailboxes are and sometimes if I need to clear my head I'll use my mail as an excuse to take a walk over there late at night, when the neighborhood is empty and dreamy and thought-provoking.

Now, on this particular night I was a third of the way through a bottle of wine when I went out. I decided to go have a look at the trash pile and in my altered state it looked even more like treasure to me than trash usually does. In the middle of the cardboard boxes and black trash bags was a perfectly good upholstered wheely chair that had arms. Holy shit, what a coup. Arms meant it was the kind of chair someone important would sit in, someone like the principal, Sister Josaphat. I had to have it. I kept walking and passed the lot briskly, playing it cool, with the idea to swoop down and grab the chair when I passed by again on my way back home.

Inside the contained quiet of the post office I heard my ears buzzing and realized I was kinda drunk. So what. Maybe it would give me the courage to trash-pick from a church like a weirdo. When I got back the chair was still there, its shape already familiar in the semi-darkness like it was waiting for me.

I stepped over the low chain strung between the gap in the fence and went over to the chair, stroked its back, the leather-looking plastic punctuated with two buttons. For an old chair it looked fine and—I gave it a sniff—it smelled fresh. Next to it in a tangle I saw some kind of paper trash that looked like discarded classroom decorations, and whatever it was I knew I had to have that too. I pulled up a handful of the papers and saw that it was a long red construction paper chain with writing on each link. Now *that* is the kind of thing I really love to find. I arranged the red chains in a drapey fashion over my new chair and started to push it away from the trash pile, then immediately stopped. The chair's hard wheels on the bumpy pavement sounded like a tank rolling down the street, and the neighborhood was as quiet as a cemetery. I looked around and didn't see anyone, but still, how was I going to get it home? It was too heavy for me to pick up and carry and I didn't see how I could make the wheels any quieter. I'd just have to push it as fast as I could. The street was on a very subtle incline and I was headed downhill, and my big purse swung from my shoulder as I pushed the chair and it began to pick up speed. It was awkward, and I chuckled drunkly to myself like a hobo as I jogged behind the stupid bockety thing. When I realized I was having to run to keep up with the chair I thought: Why don't I just ride it home?

So I rolled it onto the blacktop of the road, sat down, and started pushing like you do on a skateboard only with both my feet. And there I went, sailing noisily down the middle of the road in the middle of the night. This whole scene was so ridiculous you'd think it would have been fun, and in retrospect it is funny, but it was actually fucking difficult to keep the chair going and I was tipsy so the rough shoving I was doing made me sweaty and queasy, and I was sure I was about to get into some kind of humiliating trouble.

I can't tell you how loud the wheels sounded. The gravelly noise was splitting the night and I had the image of every person in every house looking out a window at me as I rolled by. When I got to the bigger intersection near my building I got off the chair and walked it again, telling myself that anyone in a passing car would think I was walking my bike, but let's be honest. It wasn't that dark. Anyone could see it was a nun's office chair.

There's a boy I went to school with who's a cop on the local police force, and after this little escapade I liked imagining how I would have responded to his questions if he'd seen me looking so obviously publicly drunk and stopped me while I was flying on my chair. He would want to know what I was doing, and then he'd want to know why I was taking someone's trash, although as far as I know there's nothing criminal about that. "I'm an artist!" I would say. "Well I'm a cop!" would be his answer, I guess, and then he would arrest me or charge me a fine. The kids of Holy Martyrs, all grown up. It was weird but exciting to think of it that way, to realize that I'm not the only one who grew up and turned into something.

Back at home that night I sat down on my bed to look at the paper chain and read what was written on each link. The kids of Holy Martyrs who are still kids had printed the good deeds, or community service or whatever, they'd each done. "Golf outing," "piano for church," "helped at day camp," "trimming trees." I copied down every single one in a notebook, even the duplicates ("help my grandma," "help my grandma," "help my grandma") and then I hung the chain over my bedroom closet door where I can admire it and think about it. The next day I put the chair in my storage cage in the basement. Doing that made a tremendous amount of clatter too; the damn thing is *heavy*. I don't have a use for it yet but it's okay. Eventually I'll probably find one. It was free, at least in one sense, and the truth is I hated to think of it being thrown away.

I Love You, Secondhand Junk Yard Sale Season No. 2

THIS SEASON GOT AN EARLY, IF INAUSPICIOUS, START. It's still March and there's a chill in the air, threatening the tiny snowdrop flowers everyone feels so protective and hopeful about. Nonetheless, in the classified section this week Mom and I found the first sprinkling of listings. "Garage Sale!!!" and "GIANT YARD SALE THIS SATURDAY. NO EARLY BIRDS." We were excited to get started.

Our first outing was to mom's old neighborhood and it was nothing but a couple of drive-bys. Drive-bys are when you find a yard sale in the classified section and when you get to the address you roll slowly by and take a nice big look but keep on going because the scene is too still and potentially awkward, or else it's all Beanie Babies. Mom's town is pleasant to drive around but the yard sales are hit-or-miss.

On our way to the next address we turned down a side street that had a thrift store I'd never been inside and Mom said we could stop, even though she's not a big one for thrift stores. We went in and it was good. I'd put it in the category of carefully-chosen thrift—not true antiques, but good, quirky stuff like handkerchiefs and gloves, big brooches, that sort of thing. I ended up getting a tall, narrow china mug with a bright picture of a flower stand on either side. It has a bold blue, like, foot to stand on, so the heat doesn't touch the table where you set it down.

For fifty cents I also bought a small book, an illustrated classics-style edition of Jules Verne's *Around the World in Eighty Days*, printed on pulpy paper with cockamamy cartoonish drawings every few pages. The captions say things like "A secret too crazy to believe!" I plan to tear those pages out and use them as calling cards by rubber stamping my website's address onto them. Mom is into unicorns now, or so she told me today, so she was excited to find a cool glass box with one on the top.

Propped up on a shelf next to some books was a wooden sign carved with a lake scene, a little man standing in a boat, catching a fish, which has jumped out of the water and is huge in the foregound. The word Maine is carved across the top in a fancy script. I was actually tempted to buy this plaque. We went up to Maine every summer when I was a kid. My dad's brother Charlie lived there with his family, not in one of the ritzy-rugged coastal towns but in the western part of the state, where the mountains are, near New Hampshire. Moose country, very rural. Harsh poverty and the deepest woods you can imagine. It was beautiful and it scared me a lot. It was also the only time during the year we spent all together as a family, since my dad worked so much the rest of the time. We stayed in a tiny cabin on a lake called Mitchell Pond—unless they were big the lakes up there were referred to as ponds—and it was on those vacations that Dad taught me and Liz to paddle a canoe, bait a fish hook, and, in one screamy session over the sink, to gut a fish. Some nights we'd drive to my uncle's house for dinner and on the way home we'd have to drive through deep woods. As a thrill my father would turn off the taillights for just a moment as he drove and Liz and I would turn around and stare behind us into the unbelievable darkness, scaring ourselves for fun.

After the thrift store Mom and I walked up the street a few blocks to look for the yard sale. It was such a pretty day I couldn't help but feel peppy, even a bit giddy. The air was cold and breezy, but the sky was blue and everything trembled with new life about to explode. In a cardboard box on these people's front lawn I found three records I wanted—*Combat Rock* by The Clash, *The Who By Numbers* (the previous owner connected the dots in the cover picture with a pencil), and *Endless Summer* by The Beach Boys. There was a painfully shy, sweet young teenage girl who couldn't bear to speak to us, but her dad told me the records were a quarter apiece. "Can't beat the price," my mom and I said in unison, and then the man asked if we needed a bag. "Bags are five dollars," he joked. Har har. It was nice though. As soon as I got back home Trixie and I put on the Clash album. We could hardly believe how good it sounded on vinyl. "Murder! Is a CRIIIIME!" I'm gonna play it again right now.

•   •   •

Spring is finally really here. The weather is so beautiful it's silly, and there's baby grass growing and tiny buds on the trees. I'm in the same good, light mood I was in last week, when we found the unicorn and the Clash record, which is unprecedented. I may sound like a cheerful person to you but I spent most of the winter dreaming about climbing into my own grave. Sometimes I get...ahhhh...depressed.

This afternoon the three-day sale at St. Martin's began. It's a good one. St. Martin's is in the village center the next town over, on a block of big old weatherbeaten houses. It's the church of a friend of my mother's who she's on awkward terms with, a woman she has known all her life because they grew up across the street from each other. They had a long-overdue fight last Christmas, repressed-family style, and I think I'd feel embarrassed seeing her now, though Mom assures me it would be fine. But we didn't expect to run into her today since it's a Thursday and she works, and sure enough the only people "manning" the tables were very old ladies. They were all on-the-ball and funny ladies, though. I like what I've seen of this community.

One great thing I found was a *Gregg Shorthand Manual* from the sixties in beautiful condition. I love the look of handbooks, guidebooks, textbooks, and manuals, especially ones from that era. When I got this one home I was tickled to find personal items tucked inside it: a membership card to the American Bowling Congress 1964-

65, signed Frances W—, and a fabric bookmark with a prayer on it. Looking at these things I was put to mind of my next-door neighbor Pat, a woman in her late-80s. Pat has lived in my apartment building since 1962, when she moved into her two-bedroom place with her mother, who died about 25 years later. She is brusque and always talks in the same unmodulated loud tone of voice and doesn't own a single skirt or dress—even her dress-up outfit is a slacks suit.

Pat was a secretary for the same company for her entire professional life. She got the job the year after she graduated from high school and kept it until she retired, and now she bowls competitively all winter and golfs in the warm weather. She likes to work big jigsaw puzzles which she has sometimes coated in Mod Podge and given to me to hang on my walls. She and I got into it once when I had to tell her she couldn't open my newspaper and help herself to the sports section without asking me, but I'm fond of her, and proud of knowing her in some funny way. She's as tough as a truck tire and the things she does and says amuse me. "How about a glass of the old mer-low?" she said to me once, holding the bottle up, when I was over there visiting. I don't think she would have had any religious articles like old Frances did—in fact I know she wouldn't, because she once told me that she thinks most people who go to church regularly are "no better than bums in the park." But still, this sixties-era shorthand book owned by a lady who liked to bowl, well, Frances and Pat could well have been friends.

It amazes me that from this one item, this one rummage sale find, I can get a pretty clear picture in my mind of a person I've never met and who may very well be dead by now. I love you, secondhand junk.

I also bought a set of four wine glasses in their original cardboard container for two dollars at the "fancy table." This is good because now when someone comes over I can serve them wine in a glass instead of a mug or something. The woman I paid told us that she used to run the ten-cent table and we joked about her big promotion.

The next morning, a Friday, was Our Lady of the Gossipy Ladies. It's a treat to go to one of these on a weekday, and this pretty, mid-nineteenth-century church is just a couple of doors down from the local library I use all the time, so we walked there. But sure enough the bad behavior of the women volunteering there was in evidence again. A couple of them were talking in loud voices about some unpleasant gossip, something about how "no one was surprised" about "him." However, a few minutes after we arrived I noticed a woman in her forties over in the clothing section, struggling to get a bikini top over her t-shirt, and I was like, "Yes. These eccentric rummagers, these are my people."

And oh, the finds. I made my way immediately to the shoe area and came up empty handed (footed, haha), but on the table above the shoes I discovered a great blue clutch purse made of some kind of woven fabric. It's one of those ones that snaps closed and then folds in half, like over on itself, for you to hold. It looks like it's at least 25 years old but also like it hasn't been used because the paisley-print lining fabric is completely intact. It's meant to be a daytime bag and I do believe I'll take it to the food store later this afternoon.

Another truly delightful item is a strange ceramic mug with no handle that says the word "water," very plainly and weirdly specifically. Why do you have to put water in it? But it happens to be perfect for me and here's why. I used to always bring a mug of water to bed with me in case I got thirsty during the night, and every night Trixie would stuff her head into it and start drinking the water as soon as I set it down on the bedside table, which meant that I couldn't drink any more of it. This became so predictable that I eventually started taking one big swallow and then setting the mug down on the floor so that she could just have it and not injure me by standing on my chest in order to drink from it where it sat on the table. Now the bedroom floor mug is not only an institution but it is the only place she will drink water from—she ignores her own dish in the kitchen. So when I saw this one labeled water it seemed perfect for her.

I passed by the kids' section, which was cluttered with battered plastic toys, planning to ignore it as usual when I saw Dream Phone sitting on a table. Oh, Dream Phone. What a great game that was. The idea was, a boy liked you and you had to figure out who he was by collecting cards with different boys' numbers on them and calling them up. Creepy, recorded voices that somehow did not sound at all like teenage boys, or even especially human, would give you hints about the boy's preferences in clothes and food. "He looks cool in whatever he wears!" went one beginning part, the clue following afterward in an unintentionally sinister whisper: *"He's not wearing a tie."* I think Mom might have enjoyed this game even more than Liz and I did, but we never got Dad to play with us, which we agreed would have made the experience extra hilarious. He had no sense of humor about the idea at all. I even managed to get my college boyfriend to play it with us, but not him.

The other best thing I found was a tote bag from the Jane Austen house in England. It's printed all over with blue drawings, the original illustrations from the novels Pride and Prejudice and Emma. Someone left a piece of gum or candy in the bag, some of which is still stuck to the bottom, and it stained the fabric slightly. I might put it through the wash to see what happens, but I actually don't care. It's not much of a stain.

This church has one large auditorium, where most of the rummage items are, and they also use another room that looks like an office. This is the room with just books. I found the usual kind of good stuff—a collection of Dorothy Sayers stories, a ruined copy of Peter Rabbit that I can use for the pictures, that sort of thing. Mom found two neat old gardening books that should be fun to look at, and a primordial Weight Watchers cookbook. But as I was pawing through one cardboard box I found a hardbound book with a colorful paper cover by someone named D—. R—. Why does that name sound familiar, I wondered. Then I remembered, it's the lovely man who wrote me a letter asking me a question about a book I'd reviewed for the newspaper. It's neat when things come together like that, isn't it? I read the jacket copy of these two books and the biography put this D.R. in the right geographical place, but not the right time—they were both published in the fifties. It must be his father or even his grandfather. I'm going to write him another letter and tell him. Maybe he'd like to have them.

I found a poetry book that had been given as a gift by an elderly woman I knew from church, which I know because she gave it an inscription, dated the year I was born. She was a very short and stout Italian woman with an equally short husband who was in love with my mother. They were from Italy, I mean. Once he took my mom's hand and just gazed at her face when we ran into them in the supermarket. I paid $3.50 for all of this stuff together, including the dollar they charged us for all of those books as part of their "$1 for a basket of books" scheme. Not bad.

The next morning was warm and bright, lovely but not really. I felt exposed, jangly. Sitting in the car, speckles of woozy sunlight sliding over me, I wished I was back at home on my bed with a blanket around me.

But we were going to a moving sale, and those are better than yard sales: more stuff. On our way there a fox darted across the busy street in front of our car. It was startling and beautiful. This is in suburban Philadelphia, a very congested area. I had never seen a fox before in real life.

When we got to the house, a pretty stone-and-white-painted wood one, there was an elderly woman sitting happily on a lawn chair while two mildly disagreeable middle-aged women stalked the driveway, seeming ill-at-ease. Make of this what you will.

They were selling a nice multicolored cork board in the shape of an owl, which I considered a must-have. Some foolio wrote "hello" on it in pen, followed by two words I can't make out (*hello cork owl?*) but it doesn't matter, they'll get covered up when I tack things to it. I also saw a painted metal bowl I liked with mushrooms on it that said "Made In Finland" on the bottom. The lady, one of the younger ones, charged me two dollars for it, which I felt was steep, but I paid it because she'd made up the price on the spot and had made it slightly awkward by saying defensively "I schlepped it all the way from Finland!"

The best things I got were two candleholders, matching fat, curvaceous ones made of plaster that are painted a vibrant golden yellow. Very "be our guest." Also, I can't justify it but I found a framed poster I thought was hilarious. It's a photograph of a guy wearing riding clothes, leaning against a Bentley and holding a glass of champagne with this slogan above it: Poverty Sucks. The fact that I find this stupid thing funny must have something to do with my affinity for eighties-era depictions of richness and Britishness, which I cobbled together as a kid from the *Arthur* movies, *The Fresh Prince of Bel Air*, and John Hughes' movies. Something tells me I'm not the only one.

At this point Mom and I decided we needed to refresh ourselves so we drove to our favorite restaurant, which is called Something Pizza but is actually a diner. We try to go there about once a week. It's an old-fashioned place with a striped awning on the main street that runs through our town which, if you stay on it, will take you all the way into downtown Philadelphia. When we got out of the car we noticed a couple of guys at the old shoe repair shop a few doors down. They seemed to be decorating the front window in some way so we went and had a peek. It was so neat, one guy was sitting in a chair on the sidewalk and making an old-fashioned painted sign right on the glass. At that moment he was making the white outline of a wing tip shoe and telling the man with him how he would put "since 1923" in the middle. We apologized for peering over their shoulders and complimented the work, and the painter said, "That's okay, it's beautiful!" We agreed that it was, and he said, "No, it's beautiful of y'all to come and look at it!" He told us to come by with our shoes or handbags if we needed them fixed, and we said we would as we waved goodbye.

I was starving and I wanted a cheeseburger. At the diner, Mom and I got to talking and eating and after a while this cute guy came in. He's the kind of guy I always think would be just right for me but I never actually meet them. Trim and tidy, handsome and smart-looking but not overdoing it in some smart-guy hipster get-up. I like self-possessed guys who seem like they're content to be quiet and to spend time alone, the way I do. I don't know, I just liked him. I told Mom some of this in a hushed voice as he ordered his food at the counter, and I glanced up at him as he walked out with his food and he looked at me and gave a small smile. Mom was like, "You're right, that would be somebody good for you." I could see the gears turning. "You've got to figure out the kind of place where guys like that would work. Then you can get a job there and meet them." This seemed pretty far-fetched to me but I humored her and we brainstormed good places to work. Mom suggested a law office and I just gave her a look.

After lunch we got back in the car and didn't feel like going home, but Mom pointed her car in that direction and we coasted along the streets. As we were moseying around, drowsy in the sun with the windows down, who do I see sitting on a bench and eating his sandwich in front of a row of shops but the guy. I go, "Mom! That's the guy!" She maneuvered through an awkward street hockey game that these three boys constantly have going in order to go back around the block so she could see. "You're right," she said, "that is him," sounding as disbelieving as I felt. She went slowly to read the sign in front of the building: such-and-such real estate properties. I will have to make an effort to comb my hair and look less like a hobo when I walk around town from now on, just in case I run into my future husband. I mean, do you believe it? We found out where he works!

•   •   •

Mother lode! On this rainy first Saturday of May Mom and I drove around looking for yard sales but only stopped at three, since the others we passed or had circled in the classifieds looked unpromising and embarrassing. At the first one I made the only purchase of the day: a blue "portable" Smith Corona Silent-Super typewriter in its (smelly) case—for *one dollar*. I say portable in quotes because you know those things, it weighs about 98 pounds. I wouldn't even have noticed it—I was examining a set of ceramic measuring cups that looked like owls on tree branches—but the man whose house it was piped up and went, "I guess nobody wants a typewriter!" It was shut up in its case on the driveway and I just hadn't noticed it or known what it was. When I squatted down and popped the lid open I died. It's a manual typewriter, a great looking blue metal typewriter in perfect condition, with the letters of Smith Corona in raised white plastic.

Now, I don't need a typewriter because Mom gave me one for my last birthday. It's a new one by Olivetti, a reproduction that she went to some trouble to find, and it sits on my desk next to my laptop and I use it about every day. But this one was so cool, and I happen to know that Alex Wrekk, the queen of zines, collects typewriters and owns about eight of them. So I'm allowed to have two, right?

There's something dear to me about typewriters, and I think it's because I can almost remember the time that they were useful, but not quite. When I was in grade school we had an electric typewriter in the house, but at that age I was still required to write all of my reports for school by hand. By the time I was old enough to learn to type we had a computer. Therefore the typewriter was a formerly useful thing that was now just for playing, which made it mysterious and powerful, stately with recent importance. It cracked out a satisfying snapping sound when you typed and it hummed all the time, beginning the moment you turned it on, which always made me a little nervous, like it was impatient for me to get to work.

At home I took the case down to my storage space in the basement since it already smells like a basement and I don't need it anyway. Then I tested the keys on the typewriter and they work and so does the ribbon that's in it. I love my life right now.

This day was also significant because it was the day that my mom decided once and for all that she is a rummage sale person and not a yard sale person. She gets embarrassed going to people's houses. I agree, it can be awkward. It depends. Some people have the right approach to the whole thing and are doing it because they enjoy talking to people and telling stories about their old stuff and are happy to find a new home for it. Like the typewriter guy. He was only charging a dollar for that thing and he seemed pleased that I was excited to find it. Other times people try to nickel-and-dime you for their crappy decrepit wicker plant holders and it's like, Get over it, it's a yard sale, you're not opening a g.d. boutique.

The other house we went to that day was a ten-minute drive away from home and it turned out to be unremarkable. The woman running it had her lawn chair up on the sidewalk, which seemed odd, but maybe that's where she thought she'd get the most sun. Some yard salers seem to be in it for the tan. As we browsed for a minute, mostly out of politeness, a woman from our parish came up and surprised us by being warm and friendly. Sometimes there's an awkwardness with women my mom used to be friendly with. When my dad died not everyone acknowledged it, probably because he wasn't Catholic and these people live in a very small world, and this has hurt my mom and made her wary. But this lady hugged her and I could see my mother's brittleness soften, and that was nice.

When we got there lines of tables were set up along the front perimeter of the lawn and then down the driveway and onto the sidewalk. I bought a soft pretzel from a lady on a cell phone and squirted it with a line of yellow mustard. One of my favorite treats. But I ate two bites of it and was struck with the most sudden and violent wave of nausea I've ever experienced. I covered my mouth and ran behind a brick building, fully expecting to puke on the concrete, but after a moment it passed. What a terrible feeling nausea is. Totally unique, not pain but something singularly distressing. I had no idea what caused it but Mom told me that back in the day yellow mustard was sometimes used to induce vomiting. Who knew? I hope this won't interfere with my pretzel-mustard habits in the future.

I didn't see much I wanted at the sale but then I came upon a great looking large yellow ceramic teapot for a mere one dollar. An imprint on the bottom said Waechtersbach, West Germany. So I bought that and as I carried it back to the car a man and a woman sitting together at a table hollered out compliments. About the teapot, not me.

•　　•　　•

The rummage sale at Mount Holly Methodist always takes place on a Friday instead of a Saturday. That's fine with me and Mom, since she's free during the day and I work from home. This is the place where, last year, Mom and I were amused to see an old man asleep in a folding chair by the door.

This year it was much livelier, with more people and chatter filling in the gymnasium and the church's community building. Last night I said to my mom, "I need coasters, remind me to look for coasters." I remembered and found two plastic ones that look like orange slices. They're bright colored and look like they'd feel like jelly if you pushed them with your fingertip, but they're made of hard plastic. I also found a box of taper candles and chose two lime green ones I thought would fit and look good in my new yellow candlestick holders.

Then Mom spotted a tiny tea set in a box that I hadn't noticed. She went, "Katie, would this be good for your" and then she mouthed the word "dollhouse?" Yeah, I have a dollhouse, so what? It makes a good "talking piece," as one of my neighbors said when I showed it to her, and I enjoy making things for it, such as a dining table I put together from a kit. Standing there I pictured the silent tiny dining room, with its stained-wood sideboard and white curtains. The tea set would look just right in there.

On other tables I found a rooster salt shaker, a red change purse, a sun catcher with a cardinal on it, and a small original watercolor in a frame which the artist, Judy Buswell, signed and dated "1991." Underneath the date is the artist's phone number. It was hard to resist the temptation to call a home phone number that someone has made public but I found the strength and looked for her online instead. I found her website and her bio says she quit her career as a nurse practitioner at age 40, learned to paint, launched her own greeting card business two years later and sold one million cards during her third year in business. Go Judy!

The next morning I woke up all excited. It's high season right now for yard sales and there were three neighborhood-wide ones listed in the paper for today. But ... they fell into the categories of awkward and unimpressive. I think maybe Mom and I are becoming more discerning in our rummaging, that's all. We're old hands at this point.

However, we did stop on one block that had two sales next to each other. My mom picked up a wall clock and showed it to me. "Katie, don't you need a clock for your kitchen?" I took the clock from her and looked at it for a moment—all the numbers appear opposite where they're supposed to and they're printed backwards. And the hands MOVE backwards. Yes! An old man browsing nearby said, "You get younger!" to which I responded, "Yeah, there are a few things I wouldn't mind undoing." Oops, I went too dark. I always accidentally take small talk to that next level. The woman whose house it was was German, I could tell—she spoke English with that throaty accent. She told me her son had loved the clock too and sold it to me for three dollars. I had no money on me as usual, so Mom paid. Since I owed her four dollars from yesterday too I bought lunch later at the Pizza Diner. A nice Saturday morning.

· · ·

Now this was an unusual day of yard saling. Mom and I were joined by my sister, which doesn't happen very often. Since she was with us Mom and I were emboldened to roam around less familiar city neighborhoods to check out the action there. (In general Liz is a more intrepid driver than Mom is, and I still don't know how to drive at all.) We found ourselves investigating a sale we'd seen in the classifieds in the city's posh old Chestnut Hill section, where I found an excellent zippered navy blue tote bag covered on one side in the names of cities and countries in white uppercase letters. Philadelphia is on there, represent! The words are very tidy, listed one after the other, and it's queer because cities and countries are jumbled together nonsensically. You've got both "London" and "England" but not next to each other. It's odd. I also found a delicate, old-fashioned ladies' watch in silver that works but, as I found out when I tried checking the time later, is slow. It'll need a new battery but mark my words, I won't bother doing this a new battery but mark my words, I won't bother doing this any time soon or maybe ever. The watch and the tote bag were a dollar each.

Liz found a flower press for a quarter. She's into gardening but in a less ladies-who-lunch kind of way than I am. More like, she works for the city and uses augers to plant 200-pound trees. The flower press is made of pieces of particle board with plastic clamps that tighten them together. We laughed because it says it's for children up to age 10. What? Those warnings are supposed to tell you that kids have to be old enough to use something, not young enough. Is the flower press supposed to be too childish for someone over the age of 10? How so? I'd venture to say that most people interested in pressing flowers are older than 10. Well, no one stopped her from buying it, anyway.

The people in Chestnut Hill tend to be boiled-wool, blue-blood snooty but it's beautiful there, and the other sale we went to up the block was a moving sale so we got to see inside the house. The people invited us to walk through the almost-empty rooms, which where old and great looking with elegant molding around the floors and ceilings and built-in wooden kitchen cabinets with glass doors. We didn't buy anything, just looked, and decided to scoot out when we overheard the couple disagreeing about a mop or broom of some kind that someone wanted to buy. The wife wanted to sell it but the husband, who was standing on the sidewalk getting something out of his car, wasn't going for it. "We'll never use this, will we Tom?" she called out to him. "I will," he said without taking his head out of the car's trunk.

We drove down the hill a bit till we were in Mount Airy, which also has great old rambly houses and a nice vibrant feeling. It's eclectic and old and somewhat fancy but much more down-to-earth, and comfortably diverse, ethnically and economically. I used to work with a girl who grew up there and she said it was like living on Sesame Street. We stopped at a sale a young hippie-hipster couple was having and I tried on some crazy eyeglasses. They were cool and I wanted them but they looked terrible because they obscured my eyebrows. That's no good. I don't want to look like Ziggy Stardust.

We wove through the neighborhood in Liz's hot little car and after a while we passed a full bookcase just sitting on the sidewalk. Hm. We parked to check it out and it turned out to be bait, set out there by the owner of a used bookstore housed inside the train station that was just down a small hill. I'll be damned, I never knew it was there. The store inside was big in a secret way, with several warren-like rooms, one after the other and up the narrow, winding staircase, like something out of Tolkien. I nearly bumped my head on the ceiling over the stairs. Many of the books were first editions or special things that would be of interest to collectors in some way, but plenty of them were regular old used books, affordable. How had we never heard of this place? The owner was a big friendly bearded man who offered us coffee, and a slim grey striped cat kept an eye on us as we browsed. I fell in love with a guy in long dreads and a suit who smiled at me through a doorway to another room and then I bought two books. One is a paperback book of poems called The Motorcycle Betrayal Poems by Diane Wakoski, totally seventies. The subtitle is "This book is dedicated to all of those men who betrayed me at one time or another, in hopes they will fall off their motorcycles and break their necks." The other is a beautiful hardbound book printed in 1911 called *First Lessons in English For Foreigners*. I love old spelling, grammar, and language usage books like this and can't resist buying them. The text of instructional reading books has a kind of eerie chanting poetry to it:

OPEN ONE WINDOW.
OPEN THE DOOR.

OPEN YOUR BOOK.
OPEN YOUR KNIFE.
SHUT THE DOOR.
SHUT THE WINDOW.
SHUT YOUR BOOK.
OPEN TWO WINDOWS.
SHUT THE WINDOWS.
STAND UP. SIT DOWN.

Once we were back at home we ate lunch at our diner again and I went to my apartment to be by myself. I had horrible menstrual cramps and I don't remember the last time I felt so dead tired. I looked up the bookstore on the Internet and found out that the building it's in was the original train station and was designed by Frank Furness in 1882. I looked at my books for a little while and fell asleep on my bed.

•   •   •

Wow, the middle of this summer was dumb. Sometimes it's like that. Once we get into the real slog of summer the fun things—the big church sales and flea markets—slow to a trickle, so it's just yard sales and those can be terrible. Mom and I looked in the paper faithfully every Wednesday and circled a few things, but few of the places we went to were worth stopping for. Well, there was one house that had a friendly lady and a bunch of crazy things for sale, but I am a purist and I don't think her sale counts. We talked with her a bit and found out she owns a thrift store in town and occasionally holds yard sales to try to unload some of the stuff that's not selling. So, she's a dealer. That's not the same as a person selling old family things from their basement and attic. However, I did buy a stack of awesome papers for one dollar: a laminated volunteer firefighter i.d. card from 1975, an old Western Union telegram in its original envelope, and a 1980s Christmas card from the governor of Pennsylvania featuring a terrifying Dayglo-looking photograph of his spooky little smiling-perfect family.

One other thing that happened in June: I went to the cemetery on my dad's anniversary. For several years I refused to visit that place. Not that anybody was trying to force me to, but inside my mind I was very defiant about it. I didn't see what the cemetetry had to do with my dad, and I preferred to think I have his company when I listen to his records, or look at his Charlie Chaplin poster, or come across the corncob pipe he used to smoke that I stole a million years ago to smoke some bag of weed I'd gotten my hands on. I still prefer to think that. But now I can see the purpose a place like a grave can serve for the living.

It's quiet by his grave, tucked in a little from the roaring street traffic. I pushed a bunch of wildflowers from my mom's yard into the ground with a wire hanger. The groundskeepers come through every few days and clear away the gifts people leave— the flowers and photos, teddy bears and flags — but I didn't care, I wanted to do it anyway. It felt good to to have gone to the trouble. It made me realize that this was the real tribute, not the flowers themselves. Spending some time making a gift for him, like I did as a kid, like I would have continued to do if he were still alive.

And now it's July, hot relentless humid July, the month that nobody who wasn't from here would believe how like a Florida swamp it is. It's foul. Still, there are things about the summer that are great, like the Fourth of July sale at the shore.

Every year that goes by the shore town we go to gets more built up and overcrowded. It can be hard to take. For one thing, a veneer of fake commercial cutesiness has been painted over the surface of the place, which was pretty damn cute to begin with. It's called "America's first seaside resort" and its streets are lined with ornate Victorian houses that are painted in candy colors with matching flowers in hanging baskets on their porches. You can picture it.

But there is a loveliness that was always there that's

real. I like this place, in part because I'm a Philly kid and growing up we all went "down the shore," and in part because this particular town is the kind of place that feels like autumn all year round. Do you know what I mean? It feels...old, and a little bit spooky in a delicious kind of way, with breezes swishing around corners and the feeling of spirits alive all around you. Some summers we've spent weeks down there, and other years we only get down a handful of times. For the Fourth Mom and I decided to go down the Wednesday before the holiday, which fell on a Friday this year. The firehouse bazaar was scheduled for Saturday.

Like last year and every year the town held a bazaar to benefit the volunteer fire company. They raffled off things like a sea kayak and dinners at local restaurants, and there are tables of "white elephants" lined up inside the firehouse. We love this event and look forward to it every summer, and then it ends up being sort of anticlimactic because, well, maybe we remember it as being more fabulous than it really is.

Mom and I got down to the house on Wednesday and settled in, then drove into town where all the shops are and walked around. I felt relaxed right away, which is rare for me. In town we visited the good indie bookstore that's there and the cross-stitch store, which is this fabulous place that is like spiritual for us. Mom loves to do needlework and there's nothing like this where we live. The tiny store is crammed with kits and charts for making needlework pieces, mostly cross-stitch, which I enjoy too. I bought a packet of designs that I planned to work on and, at the bookstore, a novel called *Like the Red Panda* that was on sale for like four bucks.

The rest of the weekend we had nothing planned, just puttering around, taking walks, taking the bikes out of the shed and tooling around on the back country roads if we felt like it. I read that book in a day and it left me crushed with sadness. I decided to go over to the tiny church a few blocks from our house. Mom wanted to come too, to take a picture of it to send to one of her pen-pals, who'd once sent Mom a picture of the church she goes to. That's fine. I was planning to go alone but I can feel close to alone with her. I put on a sun hat and slapped over there in flip-flops and a baggy white skirt.

The sun was bright but it wasn't very hot and not at all humid. We looked around at the houses we passed and commented on renovations and said how much better we thought it was to spruce up a pretty, modest house than to raze it and put up a huge hideous McMansion. These plots of land are so close together—and were apparently zoned for maximum money-making—that those ugly big houses look like they're trying to elbow each other out of the way.

The church is really a chapel, it's so small. It was built in the 1880s after the original design, which was built in the 1840s and then burned down. We went inside slowly, and no one was in there so we sat down. The walls are white plaster on the top half and buffed warm wood on the bottom. There are two rows of only 17 pews with a narrow blue carpet running the length of the aisle. Everything in there is perfect. The wood looks healthy and oiled but not too-shiny lacquered. There are blue hymnals in clear holders screwed to the back of each pew, and one sitting at either end of every pew like plates on a table. The kneelers were all up. Six ceiling fans with little fluted lights hung still overhead, each with two cords: one for the lights and one for the fan, I guess. The cord with the larger ball at the end hung lower than the other cord by about two inches on every single fan.

Up at the front a simple altar was dressed with a white cloth edged in gold scallops, and on either side of it stood two tall gold candlestick holders with thick white candles. They were set back against the wall and I knew that they weren't so much decorations as a part of the service. Two altar boys carry them down the aisle alongside the priest as they process in to music when Mass starts. There are no statues and there's no crucifix up front, just a few flat icon paintings in earth colors and burnished gold. It blew my mind that this church could look so perfect without striking me as fussy. Mom and I sat there quietly for a while. The whole time I had to keep myself from crying, not the kind of tears that spring to my eyes and burn them but that obey me and never reach my eyes at all but run lush down my insides instead, like a waterfall. I swear I can feel it happening. Is this what happens to you when you can't cry? I want to cry almost every time I'm in a church. I have since I was a kid, and I went to Mass every Sunday and every day went to my grade school, which was right next to the church. That's a lot of times to feel like you want to cry.

Later that night was fireworks, but we didn't know it. At around 10 Mom and I were sitting around watching TV and she said, "I think I'm going to stroll down to the beach, Beetle. Do you want to come?" We call each other Beetle, among other nicknames. This one started the summer she had a Japanese beetle infestation in her garden.

There's a quiet beach down at the end of our street. I said "okay" and put down my needlework—an art deco-style flower I was making for a friend's birthday, which I got from that cross-stitch book I told you about. I put my flip-flops on. We walked out the front door and Mom said, "Let's"—she mouthed this part for all the bandits who were hiding in the bushes—"leave the door unlocked."

It always gets darker at the shore at night than it ever does at home, and it's usually quiet, but tonight all these cars were turning off the streets between our house and the beach and turning left toward the ocean. As we got closer we saw all these people walking too, some of them carrying chairs and stuff. "What's going on, Beetle?" we wondered to each other, and I guessed maybe fireworks, even though the holiday was the next day.

We walked on the sand path beside the dunes leading to the beach. There used to be a wooden walkway but now it's hard-packed sand. There were tons of people lined up on the beach. We could hear their voices murmuring and see their silhouettes against the sky. And before we even got out onto the beach we saw something bright in the sky, over to our right. Everyone went, "Ohhh!" including us. So it was fireworks. They were far enough away that it wasn't the same effect as sitting underneath them and watching them fill the sky, but it was a good view and they were beautiful. Mom and I just stopped where we were and leaned against the wooden picket fence and rested our faces on it to watch. We stood there watching the colors and explosions without saying anything and I went to a quiet place in my mind. I love fireworks and I never get bored watching them. They went on forever, and you could tell when the big finale was happening because they popped faster and faster and made bigger spheres of color, and when they were finished everybody clapped.

My sister got up early the next morning to drive down from Philly in time to go to the bazaar with us, which started at 8:30. After those long descriptions of the church and the fireworks you're probably expecting a lovingly detailed story about the bazaar but I'm sorry, it wasn't that exciting. Liz bought a raffle ticket for the sea kayak, as she does every year—"Those things go for like 300 bucks!"—and gave her phone number in case we missed the drawing later that day, which we did. I guess she didn't win.

I love to look at the tables of books that they set up on the grass next to the firehouse. As I do every year I felt like punching people in the face because they weren't real rummagers and didn't know the etiquette—or, apparently, any sort of etiquette, because I can't think of a single social situation where it's appropriate to breathe down someone's neck until they get out of your way or bounce off of people rudely as you walk by without saying excuse me. But whatever, I have anger problems. It was fun anyway.

Outside near the book section is the food. I didn't get any but Liz bought a big soft pretzel with mustard. It looked so good to me but then I remembered the time in May when I almost threw up and didn't get one. They also had hot dogs that people were totally buying and eating at 9 AM. Summer grossness, I love it.

I saw a bunch of interesting books and Liz and I had a funny conversation with one of the women working there about this amazing set of romance novels. There was one for each state of the union, and they were all about the "Montana macho man" or "the wild one from Wisconsin." Liz and I found Pennsylvania and New Jersey and we were gonna get them, but while we were talking to that woman she told us how excited her friend was when she got her a whole series of stupid books like these from last year's sale so we decided not to break up the set. The three of us marveled at the existence and popularity of romance novels for a few minutes. "They're *dirty*, too!" I said, and the lady laughed. She was like, "I know! My friend loves them!" The only book I bought was an old book of embroidery designs, mainly because I like the instructional drawings in things like that and figured I'd use some in a zine, or just enjoy looking at them. The fiction was mostly along the lines of those romance books, but I did see a copy of *Maus* by Art Spiegelman and got my sister to buy it. I liked that book and thought she would too.

Inside the firehouse was mayhem, which is to say fairly crowded, but it seemed heinous because the acoustics in there make the sound bounce around in an upsetting way. My cat would have gone insane. Sometimes I feel like I'm part cat, since sensory stuff freaks me out so much. Liz and I didn't spend much time in there and Mom was off doing her own thing. When I ran into her she'd found a pretty jade plant and a tote bag that commemorated the bazaar. Nice! I would have gotten one too but they were 10 bucks. I did find something ridiculous that I was excited about for 50 cents: a tiny string of Halloween pumpkin lights for my dollhouse. The lights aren't lights because they don't light up, they're just made to look like a string of lights. Really cute though.

On her way down the shore that morning Liz passed a few yard sale signs, so once we'd had enough of the bazaar we climbed into mom's car and went looking for them. We found two and they were both decent. They were also different from ones at home because this place is more country than where we live, so, like, at one house we had to walk all the way up a grassy dirt driveway to the house, which was set way back from the road. On their porch I found a book about the awesomeness of the cheesy metal bands I loved as a kid, *Fargo Rock City* by the music critic Chuck Klosterman. I read a good chunk of it later that day and enjoyed his writing style and sense of humor. Also, I agreed with most of what he said about the bands. I was reminded of so much of the music I listened to when I was eleven or twelve, some of it good/bad and some of it actually good, like Guns N' Roses and Skid Row. Yeah, I said actually good. GNR had at least two good albums: *G N' R Lies* and *Appetite for Destruction*. Skid Row was cool too. I don't care if you think they're cheesy. Get over it. They wrote some catchy, pretty songs and were also legitimately bad-ass, as Chuck Klosterman reminded me—they toured with Pantera!

Anyway, we went to one other house too. I spotted a box of records for a dollar apiece and was going through them when my sister came over and said, "Kate, c'mere, there's a huge dollhouse!" Sure enough, someone had constructed a big beautiful dollhouse and set it up in the garage. The man who made it was there telling us all about how he'd started it when his kids were at home and then let it sit for years and only finished it the other weekend. If you wanted the house you were supposed to make an offer and leave your phone number, but the guy seemed to have mixed feelings about selling it. I doubt he will. It was a full house—as in, not cut in half the way many dollhouses are so that you can see the interior—

but the front opened up like French doors on hinges. The detail was gorgeous. The guy said the scalloped shingles had all been shaped by hand, and he pointed out the brick detail around the base and on the chimneys. "Those chimneys have copper flashing," he said, laughing. "My house doesn't even have copper flashing!"

Liz found and bought a ridiculous photo of two stuffed penguins dressed in formal wear and having a fancy candlelit dinner. The caption reads, "Charles and Simone enjoy a romantic evening at home." Needless to say she bought this item. We plan to hang it up at the beach house, but we haven't done so yet. I bought four records, all of which were in fine shape: *War* and *Boy* by U2 and Bruce Springsteen's *Greetings From Asbury Park*, which seemed appropriate since there we were in Jersey, living the dream.

And it's true, I'm a New Jersey apologist. I never listen to the negative stuff people have to say about it, how it's all ugly strip malls or whatever. Most of the people who say those things have never even been there. Lots of New Jersey is beautiful, and in that rural part of South Jersey there are still plenty of working farms. We bought corn and tomatoes from a road-side farm stand that day, in fact, and had them for our lunch and then again for dinner.

After we ate I rode my bike down the long back road that leads to the quiet beaches, the ones you have to go through the woods to get to. When I got there I dropped my bike in the sand and walked down closer to the surf, where I stood and watched the day grow darker and waved at the people on the ferry as it went by. I didn't know if they could see me but I did it anyway.

SO YEAH, I HAVE A DOLLHOUSE. LAST YEAR I decided to get it out of mom's storage closet and bring it to my apartment. It weighs a ton so I had to ask my sister to drive it over, but once it was at my place I could look at it a while and think about fixing it up again.

My dad built the house for me when I was five and my parents gave it to me that Christmas; they did the same for Liz the year she turned five. You can buy a dollhouse kit that comes with all the parts, but he used a book with patterns and cut the wood himself. Mom told me how they worked on the house that winter, how at night after my sister and I went to bed they'd sneak down into the basement to wallpaper and paint one little room at a time. We loved playing with the houses when we were kids, especially Liz's. Mom and dad had become more expert the second time around, so her house had extra details, like a staircase and a kitchen sink with exposed pipes.

I had a revival of interest in my dollhouse when I was around 11, at that age where you're just about to become too old for things like that so you really go for it for a little while longer. I remember the day I got my first period, I'd spent hours trying to construct a garden in the carpet next to where the house sat on my bedroom floor. My stomach had felt funny all afternoon and when I finally understood what was going on, that I'd gotten my period, I felt stupid for having played with a toy that day. For a long time after that, looking at the house made me feel vaguely embarrassed. But no more! I've been bleeding monthly for almost twenty years now and I figure I'm allowed to play with anything I want.

I set up a work area in my living room and cleaned the dust off the roof and the shiny wooden floors. The original wallpaper was the only thing that was really ruined by time and needed replacing. Without thinking about it I figured I could use leftover scraps of real wallpaper, but picture it: If you tried that it would look terrifying, with huge flowers blooming nauseous on the walls, or big parrots like predators. Everything in a dollhouse has to be done to the same scale or it will look crazy, like an *Alice in Wonderland* hallucination. So I found and ordered wallpaper made especially for dollhouses— in the bathroom teensy seashells line up neat along the top near the ceiling—and put it up with paste and smoothed out the bumps, just like in a real house.

Then I went shopping for what the miniatures dealers call accessories. In the catalogs I browsed online I found tiny sewing machines, spinning wheels, and quilting racks you could get if you decide your dolls are into needlework. You could make a baby's nursery or a colonial-era kitchen, or decorate the whole place for Christmas or Halloween. I even found an entire category called Egyptian, as in the ancient one: You can buy a painted sarcophagus, thrones, and god and goddess figurines. When I first saw these they struck me as supremely strange, but hey. This whole hobby is pretty weird. May as well go whole hog. For my house I bought a clear goldfish bowl with "water" and a "fish" inside it, blue-and-white checked napkins for the kitchen table, an Oriental rug, and a roll top desk that slides open and closed. I still had some good things leftover from childhood, like a porcelain-looking vase that has a red and gold design of cranes and lotus flowers. It looks just right with the rug.

Then I started thinking about who should live in the house. There is a difference of opinion regarding dolls that divides the dollhouse community, I soon found out. Some people feel the people look distracting, since they can't really interact with the objects and they're so often awkward and clunky looking. Others think it's a necessary detail. Like, what's the point of a house with no one to live in it? I knew I wanted some dolls for my house, but not like the kind I had growing up, the dorky mom and dad and kids with their plush bodies and (somewhat) bendable limbs. You could sit them down on the furniture, but they looked terrible, stiff and rigid. Eventually they would slump over onto their sides, ruining the dignity of the perfect scene around them.

I found the website of a shop in Indiana that carries "contemporary" dollhouse dolls—detailed figures made of hard resin that are really charming and real-looking. I had a nice phone conversation with the woman who runs the store and ordered two young women figures from her, thinking it would be cool if my unconventional family was two grown sisters who lived together. Somehow the idea of a mom-and-dad style family made me feel weary. One of the dolls stands with her hand on her hip, a little sassy, and the other one is mid-stride, like she's perpetually on her way somewhere.

The dolls arrived in the mail a week or so later; when I took them out of their box they had a surprising heft to them, which I found touching somehow. I held them and pressed my fingers over their details—their eyebrows and elbows, the seams on their jeans and the wrinkles on the backs of their knees. Later I emailed the woman and told them how lovely I thought they were. "I was thinking of you and your dolls today," she wrote back. "I knew you'd love them."

And I do love them. They look like real people, only perfect. I named them Lily and Hyacinth van der Spiegl, Lily and Hyacinth because I like flower names for girls, and van der Spiegl because it means "from the mirror," which sounds like magic to me, and because who doesn't want to have a last name with three words in it? Once they had names stories about them started forming in my mind, and most of their biographical details were a satisfying kind of wish-fulfillment. Like, I've always had this romantic idea that I could be a lexicographer, so I decided that should be Lily's job. Lily the dictionary editor, organized and brisk, always on her way to someplace important. It was so easy, making it up, just like when I was a kid. I got almost giddy, remembering this thing I'd forgotten: If you want to do or be something you can just *pretend* to do or be it. It's practically as good, I swear.

Indecent, Dowdy, Hideous, Quaint:
Yard Sale Season No. 3

OH JEEZ, WHY AM I SO EASILY IRRITATED? Sometimes I can't help it. The women volunteering at St Martin's had loud voices and while I was in the check-out line in the church hall's kitchen one of them barked something at me about college—they were in the middle of a lively conversation about their kids—and then didn't listen to what I said in response. I tried to be polite but it probably came across as imperious. I had a mild migraine, not a blinding one but still, the pain of those is so nasty and singular, it felt like an ice pick stuck *thwack* into my temple behind my right eye. And I was feeling sad and sluggish too, because my downstairs neighbor, the super, who was diagnosed with stomach cancer last year, died this week. I guess I answered my own question.

This day wasn't all bad though. I like it over at St Martin's. It's a Lutheran church, and I listened to the women talk about their new minister, sounding proud. He's a German man named Sonntag, which I thought was a sweetly appropriate name for someone in his position. It means Sunday. Plus, I found a lot of loot here in this basement, which on this early spring day felt as cool and damp as a root cellar.

There was the brown plastic contraption called a Speedy Speller, which I had to get. I get a kick out of special books and other tools that are supposed to make spelling easy. What is the big deal? Get a dictionary. This thing has a dial on the front, and to look up a word you move the pointer to the letter of the alphabet you want, then push a bottom to make the top flip up to reveal, well, a dictionary...a very abbreviated one. I tried to look up effect, a word that is commonly confused with affect, but it wasn't even in there. Effective was though. Not very, say I!

The best find of the day was a manual typewriter, with a spool of fresh-enough ribbon still in it, for only two dollars. Holler! Maybe I should cool it with the typewriter buying. I now own three. This one is gorgeous though, a big beige tank of an Olympia. The hinges on its case are busted and it smells bad, so I think I'll chuck that, at least. The only thing written on the machine says *Made in Western Germany*, so I'll look online to find out when it was made. I'm thinking the sixties.

Inside a red wooden box on another table I found a big stack of papers with one of two different scenes on their fronts, printed in inappropriately garish colors: a mill with a waterwheel, and a thatched cottage on a country lane. These are single sheets so they're not cards, but they're printed on paper that is too lightweight to function as a postcard. Weird though they were I bought a thick stack of them, since I'm always collecting paper for pen-pal letters. In fact in another part of the basement I found a bunch of old greeting cards and flipped through them all, taking "Happy New Year," "Thanks to All of You" (that one has glitter on it!), "Friendly Thoughts," "A Sweet New Baby," and a crazy old die-cut valentine from the fifties. This features a boy in a football uniform with fuzzy hearts on either side of his head, and though it's obviously meant for a child ("For a Good Little Boy"), the sentiment inside is riddled with what sound to me like double entendres.

> YOU'VE GOT ME RUNNING 'ROUND & 'ROUND
> BECAUSE YOU REALLY RATE
> AND SINCE YOUR HEART
> IS NOW MY GOAL
> I CAN'T FORGET THE DATE.
> I HOPE TO MAKE A
> "TOUCH DOWN" SOON,
> DEAR LITTLE FRIEND OF MINE,
> 'CAUSE I'M CONVINCED
> THAT YOU WOULD MAKE
> A "SCORING" VALENTINE.

I mean, it sounds dirty, right?

Let's see, what else. I found what seems to be the pocket-size version of a card game from the let's-talk-about-it eighties—a mutation from the let's-go-into-analysis seventies, I guess. It's called the *Ungame: Couples Version* and it calls itself the "World's Favorite Self-Expression Game." It's just cards with discussion prompts that would make for one dreary evening, let me tell you. They say things like *complete the statement* "An emotional need I have at this time in my life is ..." and say *something about divorce.* Sounds like fun. I'm going to try to make poems out of them, I think. As always, I found shoes, this time a pair of substantial navy blue pumps from the late seventies or so. They have chunky wooden heels and look to me like dress-up shoes for people who don't like to get dressed up, which I think was everyone in the seventies except for people who liked disco. They're too big for me but I think I can make it work with some ugly thick knee socks. Always a good look.

I snapped up one of those bright blue Pan Am flight bags, also from the late seventies, I'd say. It's an old design but is in such good condition I wonder if it's new, like a reissue. Carrying lunch boxes and small luggage like this as a purse was popular in the nineties, so maybe they brought these back briefly.

On the table of crafts and sewing notions—can I interrupt myself here to say how touching I find it that these church sales use the same tables for the same things year after year? Who is it who remembers *No, this is where the tools and appliances go?* But of course I remember, so why wouldn't they? It lets me treat the sales like a store, since I always know where the kitchen, clothing, jewelry, and craft sections will be.

Like, in this case the fabric and crafts supplies were on one half of the cafeteria table nearest the stage, where they always are, and this year I found a large applique of a basket of fruit. All the fruits, the apples, pear, orange, strawberries,

and their leaves, are covered in sequins, except for the two
bunches of grapes, one purple and one green, which are done
in beads. I love this. If I were better at sewing I could make
it into a clutch purse, like the applique could somehow be the
whole front piece of the bag. But somehow I know I would
make a mess of that. Would it be boring if I just sewed
it onto a plain white tote bag? I'll have to give this some
thought.

Besides the shoes I didn't find any clothing I wanted
to buy, but I want to tell you about the handwritten sign
I saw stuck to the wall near the wheely racks of dresses.
"Designer Ensembles by the Eagle's Eye," it said. Oh, thank
you, rummage sales. Just—thank you.

That evening my friend Siobhan came over and we
went to a couple of the scabby suburban bars around here
and talked, mostly about my neighbor who'd died, and drank
beer. When we got back to my apartment there was a wooden
podium in the hall next to my door. The man who died, his
girlfriend said I could have this podium if I wanted it when I
was helping her sort through his things in the basement, and
I half liked the idea but I kept not taking it. She'd left it in his
now-unlocked storage area for me and every time I thought
of going down there to get it, seeing his half-used paint
cans and other stuff, his huge red-tasseled table lamps with
statues of toreadors on the base that Chick once said made
his place look like "a Puerto Rican bordello"—whenever I
thought of it my mind went blank and I found I couldn't do
it. So Janet had brought it by and just left it, I guess, which
filled me with irritation and tenderness and grief all at once.
"I guess this is mine now," I told Siobhan, who has always
had a pleasingly droll way of accepting sadness herself. It's
one of the reasons I like her. I picked it up and carried it
inside, it wasn't heavy at all. Siobhan sat on the couch with
Trixie and the two of them pretended to listen attentively as I
pretended to lecture to them while standing at it. It's a pretty

piece of furniture but it sure isn't very useful.

• • •

Like St. Martin's, James Memorial is a rummage sale Mom and I go to every year. In fact, they do this one twice a year, once in the spring and later again in the fall. Where do they store everything that isn't sold in the first one? Do they give it all away and just set about collecting more, like a team of single-minded magpies?

This church is in a neighborhood one town over from ours, and it's just one of many lovely old Protestant churches in this area that I'd be willing to bet has a seriously dwindling congregation. The only people who seem to keep these communities going are the old ladies. A friend of mine once suggested I conduct interviews with the women who organize the rummage sales, but this friend hosts a radio show and that's how she deals with subjects that interest her, by making them into reports. I think I'm content to fade into the background, just be another rummager, observing.

The ladies had filled their church's basement with battered wooden tables in the usual arrangement: electronics and appliances up on the stage, tiny hills of jewelry on a dresser with a mirror behind it, holiday decorations propped up in the deep wells of the windows, and rows of tables with mounds of moldering clothing filling the center of the room. I never give these clothes much of a look. It's too much trouble and too easy to make a mess, and you usually only find pilly sweatclothes and badly-shaped jeans. I will look at anything that's hanging on a rack, though, and this time I found a few winners: a black cotton dress with princess seams that I eyeballed and thought would have a nice, close fit; an oversized sweater in a grey-and-black cheetah print, and a blue sweater made of silk-like linen, loosely knit so as to be ever-so-slightly see-through. This one should look good on a spring evening with dark-colored shorts and, if I'm in the right mood, my black work boots. If not, low-heeled pumps, espadrilles, or wedges should work.

I felt curious about the fit of the dress, though, and I decided it was time to fully embrace my fate as a kooky rummager with no sense of private-versus-public behavior. I looked around and saw that no one was really watching me, then pulled the dress over my head. I yanked at the back of it, trying to get the zipper to reach.

"It's too tight, isn't it," I said sadly to a middle-aged lady nearby. She was wearing an apron with pockets for money so I figured she worked there. She had a kind face.

"Mmmm, no, I think it's fine," she said, and came over to stand behind me. She did the zipper, then tugged at the straps in the back and felt the waist, and I got goosebumps like I always do when someone nice touches me. "I mean, we used to wear stockings and girdles every day!" she said. She meant we as in women, not us two because we were both too young to remember that. I thought that was an interesting way to say it and to look at it, we as in womankind, and I liked her for it, for including me.

The sale had started the evening before and this day was the bag sale, so the usual sleepy, eccentric vibe a rummage sale has was shot through with a current of anxiety as disposophobics from all over the area stuffed as many items into their paper bags as they could: Whatever you can fit in there you can have for $2.50. So after I found those clothes I, too, kept on stuffing. I got a copy of that *Culture Jam* book by the *Adbusters* editor, which is one of those books I feel like I should have read by now but haven't. I also found Song, Speech, and Ventriloquism, a science book about the human voice for children published in the sixties. I should be able to use lines from it to make found poems. I also snagged a roundish black pleather purse with long arm straps, a rainbow belt, and two jack-o-lantern "candles" that glow plastic-orange when you plug them in. Trixie the cat and I consider things like this to be appropriate home decor all year long. Trixie is black so you can understand why she favors the Halloween look.

I didn't have much to do with the rest of my day, as I often don't on a Saturday, so after Mom dropped me off at home I decided to do laundry. I dragged my hefty sack down to the basement and was startled by a man who was on his way through our part of the basement to the door that opens onto the street. My building is actually four small buildings that are attached underneath, through the basement, which is helpful for shortening a walk when the weather is bad, but I don't often avail of this because I feel a little scared down there.

"Hello." It was just Mark, a mild, pleasant man from the C building with a ducked head and the apologetic attitude he always wears when he runs into me in the laundry room. Maybe he can tell I'm always a little scared. I said hello back and after he left I stood dropping my dirty clothes into the washer and thinking about Chick, about how I'd been seeing ghosts, practically. I was so used to bumping into him around the building that I still expected to, which had the unsettling effect of making me miss him in a practical and day-to-day way, a way I had never consciously missed my own dad, whose death had gutted me. I'd always had the sense that this was a second life for Chick, who was almost seventy when he died. I knew that he'd been a drinker and had ripped through a few marriages and made a mess of his relationships with his kids, one of whom had died and another who he'd lost touch with, but in my life he was harmless and even helpful, often giving out unsolicited advice on cleaning and fixing things as well as about relationships and other major life issues. He had a crackly, shambolic hobo energy and hoarded hulking pieces of furniture in the basement: a born superintendent. He acted in community theater, did a sort of terrible Elvis baritone when he sang, and told me his dream was to play a famous Jack Nicholson part, like McMurphy from *One Flew Over the Cuckoo's Nest*. "Now that's a guy I can relate to!" he said that time, and made a crooked grin—I know he loved having me as an audience—his Philly accent in full effect, both self-aware and not at all, as he always was. I don't understand why I miss him as much as I do.

•   •   •

I woke up with one of my headaches. It's damp and bright outside and those are the kinds of conditions my headaches need to really blossom. It wasn't a very bad one, as migraines go, and I like to think that dosing myself with caffeine via four cups of coffee was what saved me, but the truth is if it were that easy to get rid of these things I'd never get as sick with them as I sometimes do. I wanted to feel better because I was determined to get to two rummage sales this morning, one we've gone to several times before and one that was new to us.

Emmanuel Lutheran was the new discovery. I've been past it many times on the bus on my way over here to do some shopping though and I've noticed it sitting there on the corner, stone-gothic and pretty, but small. I love this part of the city. It has colonial buildings and some Revolutionary War history, so it's full of that static-y spirit energy that always makes me feel like I have company, even when the street is empty.

Mom and I picked our way through a wrought-iron gate and a pokey garden to the church's basement, which was small and quiet, with tables around the edges of the room and in a square in the middle. Not a lot of stuff but we took our time. I found a stationery set from the eighties, writing paper with a pretty pastel drawing of strawberries and a mixing bowl. It came in a folder that has a nicer drawing than the paper does—a completely different drawing, which seems odd. It's a kitchen scene, with radishes, peppers, a mushroom, a cutting board, blocks of cheese, a mortar and pestle, and a big pepper grinder, all the most picturesque kitchen stuff, all in blush-reds and butter yellows, with the strawberries and mixing bowl on the back. In the center is a plaque that reads The Nicest Days Are Mixtures of Friendship, Beauty, Joy, and Love! and I find it incredibly odd that the paper has no such slogan. Ah well. I'll enjoy writing pen-pal letters on it. I've been into that lately. When my in-person social life is busier I have less interest in writing to people, but I'll go through months of being content to connect with the human race almost exclusively through the mail.

On another table, propped up in a cluster of junky office supplies, was a nice-looking easel, a big wooden one with a cork board on the front. Mom envisioned it as a place to put a daily to-do list for Trixie, since she's supposed to be my writing assistant but hasn't been pulling her weight, to be honest. When she's not sleeping she's drowsing. I think instead I'll bring it to zine fests and tack up a price list since I find that some browsers feel shy about asking how much things cost.

On the jewelry table I made an excellent find. Can I say that the jewelry at these things is usually terrible for some reason? I never wear much jewelry but I tend to have the same taste in it as I do other things. I like it to look pretty and unusual and I opt for obviously inexpensive rather than "good." Not necessarily oversized or hideously outdated, though when I was younger I did favor this look. As you get older dressing in that jokey way starts to lose whatever cuteness it may once have had, I think. Anyway, I always expect the jewelry at rummage sales to appeal to me the way the other things there do, but it rarely does. It's all heaps of crummy silver chains and heavy clip-on earrings. And the old ladies there will tell you you'll get used to those if you wear them a lot but forget it, they hurt.

However, on this occasion as I pushed around the piles of metal and plastic I saw something I liked, a pretty pin of bright orange tulips. It seems to be a picture printed on some kind of heavy paper and then coated in plastic, making it shiny and hard. I continued sifting and found the same kind of pin with a blue morning glory on it and then another one, a hot pink lily. I am delighted with these flower pins. I'm thinking of attaching them to a small handbag all in a bunch, maybe. It's hard to wear pins, I find, unless you can rock a blazer, but those look so cloddish on me.

When we were ready to leave Mom and I approached a lady in a baggy Emmanuel Lutheran t-shirt and I showed her the things in my arms. She said, "Just pay whatever you think is fair." *What!* I panicked. This is the kind of potentially guilt-inducing situation that can spoil a day's rummaging. I gaped at her and turned to my mother, who said, "How about this?" and handed the woman a five. As we left the church Mom mused that they had a good idea asking people to name their price. We probably would have paid much less than five dollars ordinarily, the way those things are usually priced. I can't say I disapprove of their approach, but I wouldn't like rummaging nearly as much as I do if this were the way the sales always worked. I love paying next to nothing but I wouldn't enjoy getting a "deal" by being cheap with a church. And besides, I get such a kick out of lining up to check out and having a woman look at a careful price tag and add up my purchases on a calculator, with an air of seriousness, to the grand total of about two dollars. It's like we're all little kids and we're playing store.

Back outside we saw a tent. A baked goods tent! Mom bought a loaf of zucchini bread and a baggie of six chocolate chip cookies. The big, animated man behind the table—I was surprised, it's never a man—joked with us about how one cookie is never enough, et cetera et cetera, and the chit-chat exchange went back and forth a dangerous number of times, creating an irresistible force of friendliness. We disengaged more or less safely and made it back to the car, where I ate five of the six cookies within ten minutes and for a moment felt truly physically terrible, but it was worth it.

My mom's up-the-street neighbor Joan belongs to a Presbyterian church that has a decent sale twice a year, the Gossipy Ladies one. She's an odd duck, Joan. It's obviously hard for her to be social because she can never look you in the eye for more than a second, and she's capable of pretending not to see you when she passes you on the sidewalk during one of her long, galumphing walks. But she is in her true element at church. She's a deacon, or a warden, or something like that, and whenever we see her over there she perks up brightly and seems to find it easy to talk to us, which is sweet to see.

We go to their sale every time they have it, although some of the women we see there look mean and scary. They're busybodies and I can see the gears turning as they try to figure out who Mom and I are and whether we're worth being nice to. I don't care for this sort of thing but it never really surprises me. It's pretty common for people to live in a small, small world.

The sale here is okay, never earth-shattering, but it's pleasant to poke around the dim basement for a while. The woman staffing the shelf of jewelry and knick-knacks watched us admire two tiny brown ceramic animals, a snail and a quail that matched each other in an interesting way, like one was the same shape as the other only inverted. "Oh, aren't those cute?" she said. "I like to put things like that in the pots with my houseplants," which seemed like a good idea to us so we took them—the snail for me, the quail for Mom.

In the clothing area I found nothing except a slinky black skirt with a subtle silver tiger print shimmering in it like a hologram. A little cheap, you might say, but first of all it was a bigger size than I wear so I could envision it hanging off my hips and not clinging to my butt too much, and I'd wear it with an old t-shirt and sneakers which tends to take the edge off the floozyishness of clothes like that. Or so I tell myself.

Out in the hallway we bumped into Joan and chatted for a minute. She admired the skirt with a certain kind of smile—not an unkind one, just one that said, Hey, go for it while you still can, which embarrassed me so I decided not to get it. I felt stupid, thinking of Joan picturing me running around dressed like a tart. Why I care what my mom's neighbor thinks of my style of dress I couldn't tell you, since I like to think I'm more of a badass than that—and also because, as Mom reminded/reassured me on our way out the door, Joan's daughter dressed like a "streetwalker" when she was in high school. This set off another wave of anxiety in me: Did *I* look like a streetwalker in high school? Do I now? I have no ability to accurately gauge how I might appear to others so I always assume the absolute worst. But the fact is I already have a closet full of skirts I haven't been brave enough to wear outside of a bedroom fashion show with Tee, so I put this one back on the rack and we just bought the snail and quail, 50 cents for both. Then we went across the street for lunch at our diner, and we set our snail and quail out on the table to keep us company while we ate. For a few more hours the migraine stayed stuck in my temple—I had the image of a freshly sharpened pencil—and then the pain just slipped away.

.   .   .

Old Man Bread got its name last year, when we saw it listed in the paper and I tried to remember which church it was, thinking it was the one that sells day-old bread and bagels along with rummage junk, and where there was once an old man asleep on a folding chair by the door. "Is it the old man? Bread? One?" I asked Mom as I tried to puzzle it out, and we died laughing. It's not that funny but I guess but we're simpletons.

There is something very pleasing about a weekday rummage sale. It makes the experience feel just as pokey and quiet as it should. The only people in the room are likely to be me and my mom, the old women volunteering there, and one or two other kooks. Old Man Bread, which we always go to on a Friday, is an especially drowsy event. The hall where they hold it is only a small room with gymnasium floors and especially bleak lighting, and they're never selling much of anything, though the craft supply section is decent. In a big heap of linens I found a bolt of heavy cotton fabric in a marvelous lime green color. It feels like canvas but it's not quite that thick. As I caressed it Mom came over to offer me a glass bottle she found, the kind with a wide mouth for serving wine. "Or you could put an arrangement in it for garden club," she said. Which one do I like better, flowers or wine? Depends on my mood, I guess, and the time of day.

But the best finds were oddball paper goods, which is my favorite category of oddball items. I was fascinated and repulsed by an eighties-era deck of health-conscious playing cards, so I bought it. Each card has a picture of a different food on it with its calorie count underneath. Rather than nice drawings they feature unappetizing photos of different foods, cake and pretzels and, like, a plate of spaghetti. These I will mail to my pen-pals, one at a time, until they're gone.

From the same era and mindset is a small booklet called Aerobics *Fitness Plan: Stay Fit Forever!*, and underneath that one was Mixing and Serving Drinks from 1963. I got both books, though I daresay I'll find the drinks one more useful. I'm not against the idea of getting more exercise but the aerobics book says right on its first page that I should cut alcohol out of my diet completely, so this could get confusing. If I use both books will I disappear? The illustrations in both look good to me but in different ways.

The sixties book is cute, while the eighties one appeals but is mostly absurd.

Which reminds me of something I found in a book recently, and would like to reproduce for you. It's a "Fashion Timeline" by James Laver, a fashion historian, and I came across it in *The Thoughtful Dresser*, an intellectual, feminist, bright-spirited book about women and clothing.

THE SAME COSTUME WILL BE:
INDECENT 10 YEARS BEFORE ITS TIME
SHAMELESS 5 YEARS BEFORE
OUTRE (DARLING) 1 YEARS BEFORE
~SMART~
DOWDY 1 YEAR AFTER ITS TIME
HIDEOUS 10 YEARS AFTER ITS TIME
RIDICULOUS 20 YEARS AFTER ITS TIME
AMUSING 30 YEARS AFTER ITS TIME
QUAINT 50 YEARS AFTER ITS TIME
CHARMING 70 YEARS AFTER ITS TIME
ROMANTIC 100 YEARS AFTER ITS TIME
BEAUTIFUL 150 YEARS AFTER ITS TIME

If you are like me you will test these laws in your mind, using clothes you own, images of actors in movies, the fashions of various pop music scenes, and so forth as a gauge—and I bet you'll find it always works. The only variable is in the way that you personally relate to things you find dowdy, hideous, ridiculous, or quaint. I like the bad adjectives in complicated ways that I'm sure I don't need to explain to you, reader of a book about yard sales.

On the same table was a postcard postmarked 1932 that belongs in the charming-romantic category. Mary wrote in elaborate script to her friend Mrs. W.B. Rogers about her trip to Chatham, Massachusetts. "We are having one grand trip and do hope you have just as nice a one as we are having." Also found a pack of invitations to a Thanksgiving party. I've never heard of a Thanksgiving party but I wouldn't be against throwing one.

Mom got a small basket that she plans to use as a planter for garden club events. I guess she's got garden club on the brain. Incidentally, we paid a total of $1.20 for mom's planter and my stuff together. I dug in my change purse and handed her sixty cents. She looked at me like, *Uh, okay, I don't need this handful of change*, but I can sometimes be very scrupulous about paying for my rummage sale items.

The next morning I took my sweet time getting out of bed, then began the process of making coffee. It's a new thing for me to be so painstaking about it, or about anything in the kitchen—I've never gotten enjoyment out of cooking so I tend to keep it quick and simple. But bit by bit over the years I have adopted new elements to my coffee ritual, usually after I've had an especially nice cup at someone's house and asked them how they made it. These days I take a handful of beans and whirr them in the grinder I asked for for my birthday. Once those are ground down a bit—but not too fine—I put them and some water in my hefty little metal percolator and cook it up on the stove. This makes about one and a half very strong cups of coffee, and currently I'm using these Ethiopian beans that smell like flowers.

I got dressed and drank my sweet coffee with Tee, waiting for Mom to call to say she was on her way. We were planning to hit a couple of yard sales that morning, which was becoming less usual for us. As we get more seasoned at this rummaging business we often skip the yard sales and wait for the bigger sales at churches instead. Yard sales are just so *awkward* sometimes. I honestly don't know what some people are thinking. It seems to me you should be friendly and easy-going if you're going to invite the general public to your *house* via *the newspaper*, yet somehow a lot of these folks are *all business*. What is the point, if you're not having fun? To make a grand total of nine dollars? Maybe it's living in

Philly, I don't know. People here are so grumpy all the time.

Nonetheless, the first place we went to was kind of interesting. This was obviously a household of people who love old things. The garage door was open and inside sat a gorgeous old white Porsche, which was not for sale, and a gigantic jukebox, which was. Other neato things included old games in their original boxes, including a chemistry set; a white lab coat of the kind the men will wear when they come to take me away; and a pretty pair of ancient brown ice skates, their leather battered and worn like an old catcher's mitt. But the two women there were hard to engage. They just gaped at me and Mom when we said hello, and they had set prices for the jewelry that seemed too steep, from $35 to $50. It's becoming clear that I have somewhat strict ideas about how people should behave while holding a yard sale, but I really think that if you're certain something is worth that much you should sell it to a dealer. I came here with three bucks in my wallet, dude. Work with me.

But the one thing I did buy is fabulous. It's a catalog from 1971 called *Ideabook*, with a picture on its cover of a smiling woman in full big-sunglasses seventies regalia. She's tilting her head glamorously to one side and sweeping her hair away from her face with her hand, the very image of drag queen femininity. In the background is her brood, a rugged lumberjack-poet man in casual pants with a little girl on his shoulders. They're in a field and the photo's color wash is so weirdly golden it looks like the Serengeti. I love this picture. If I could climb inside it I would.

This is not a regular catalog, however, but something called "Green Stamps." Mom lit up when she saw it and had to explain to me what it was. She said you used to get stamps when you bought food, which you could paste into a book that you would eventually redeem for household items, like a set of dishes or a typewriter. Then she got a faraway look.

"When your father and I got married grandmom gave us a stamp book with stamps already in it to put toward a vacuum cleaner," she said, meaning his mom, who was never very nice to her. But still, isn't that sweet? My catalog has photos of guys playing guitars (you could order any of the clothes they were wearing and the guitars if you had enough stamps); little girls in knee socks; women lounging catlike on the floor to talk on phones; the family from the cover walking toward a picnic lunch on the Serengeti, which was being served in clear Thermalene casserole dishes; space-age table lamps; and many living rooms featuring ultrachic, super ugly home decor in beige, orange, and avocado green. To my mom these rooms are not ugly. They represent the lush lifestyle of brown shag fabulosity that she and my dad could not afford in 1971, which was the year they got married. She smiled kindly at her silly former self as she told me as much, but I could see in her eyes she still thought the stuff looked great.

The pages for pasting in stamps have tips and reminders on them. One is a line drawing of a woman with a beehive doing the calculations by holding her pen against her mouth: "When you fill this page you're half way!"

The other house we visited was also a little unusual. To get there Mom drove on back roads, trying to avoid traffic, which I love. We flew around curvy streets with no sidewalks, overgrown with bushes and tangled vines. On roads like this I want to be a passenger forever. Since I don't drive I'm usually stuck taking the bus, which I actually enjoy, but it never takes these pretty routes.

When we found the place it was an old stone house, sedate and classy, but the older woman there was animated and talkative. She told me her philosophy of keeping things moving, in and out. "I told a friend of mine whose husband just died, I said, Sometimes it's good to get rid." When she talked she sounded a bit like an actress in a black-and-white movie. I bought a set of candy dishes from her—plastic ones, but they're pretty with Art Deco scenes of the months of the year, their names in French. The other thing I found was a record called *Steppin' Out* by a seventies disco-funk group called High Energy. The cover shows the four lovely black girls in the group acting out a scene of opening the door to a guy who's there to take one of them on a date. They look fantastic in tight, high-waisted jeans and jazzy-looking sweatshirt tops, newsboy caps over soft, big-curled perms. The record inside looked too scratched to play but I wanted it anyway.

"I'm buying this primarily for the fashion," I told the lady, and she just nodded. She got me.

•　　　•　　　•

Another Catholic rummage sale! I'll be damned. I'd guess that there are more Catholic congregations in this area than Protestant ones, and as many synagogues, but only the Protestants seem to participate in this culture of rummage. But last week in the paper we found an ad for a sale at St. Timothy's, a parish church a few miles away. Mom and I have greatly enjoyed seeing what our local church communities are like, but as for exploring the Catholic ones, mostly you don't get to. Unlike Protestants, who I'm pretty sure are encouraged to try out different congregations, Catholics themselves must attend the parish church that is assigned to them geographically, serf-of-the-manor-style. Sometimes you go to a funeral but that's about it. When we saw a chance to go poking around someone else's church we jumped.

And let me tell you, this place was hoppin'. The hall was large and packed with colorful junk and people—people squeezing past each other, squatting down on the floor and trying on shoes, holding up weird things and chuckling to themselves, or calling out advice to strangers on how best to clean an otherwise useful item that's gotten kind of grungy.

This is rummaging in its purest, most powerful form. I stood and admired the scene for a moment before becoming a part of it. Most often at these events it's quieter, and I sort of mince around the room pointing at things and commenting on them softly to my mother. Today, I rummaged.

I got a stack of floppy learn-to-read picture books published in 1974. The psychedelic colors are fantastic and so are the titles, especially when read all at once. *An Apple, Dan Drum, The Dump Truck, The Pump, The Stars, The Sun and the Sand, The Drum and the Hammer, Tip Top, The Popper That Did Not Stop, Hiccups.* I found a yellow candle holder just like the lovely fat curvy ones I bought a few years ago. I also found a red tea kettle with an elegant, curved spout. I asked for a new tea kettle at Christmas, since my old one had gotten funky and lime-scaled. My sister kindly got me one, but it's a glass one and this is a problem with my electric stove. I have to put down a piece of metal between the stove coil and the kettle and I'm afraid I'll forget to do so and the thing will explode. This red metal kettle will put my fretful mind at ease. Plus, in its red curviness it looks like a tea kettle should, if you know what I mean. It's like a symbol of kettledom, like the way there's a picture of an old-fashioned handset on the call button of your cell phone, which itself looks nothing like a phone.

After the sale Mom and I stopped at the food store. When I got home I felt too lazy to take two trips, so I carried all my packages at once up the two short flights of stairs to my apartment — the lazy man's burden, my grandmother used to call it. Needless to say I tripped up the top step and fell down hard on the floor. *Shit.* I burned my leg against the rough carpet and my bags smashed on the ground. My knee hurt so bad I sat there hugging it to my body for a while. When I finally limped inside I got a floppy bag of frozen corn from the freezer and held it there. It was already looking bruised and skinned, like a ten-year-old's knee. I went back out into the hall for my bags and saw Trixie sitting there sniffing the air, feeling her freedom at being out of the apartment. I'd left the door open. "That's fine, but you're going back inside in a minute," I told her. I looked in my bags and found I'd chipped the candle holder when I dropped it. Dammit. I got down on the floor and rooted around on the carpeting until I found the big chip, which I think I'll be able to glue in place with no problem. However, there is another small piece missing still and it's pretty obvious because the white plaster is so striking against the warm color of the paint. Oh well. When things are on top of my tall bookcase I'm too short to see them properly so I guess I'll keep it up there.

The injury ended up being worse than a skinned knee. I woke up the next morning with my back completely seized up. This happened once a couple of years ago and I saw the doctor, who gave me muscle relaxers to stop the muscle from jumping and clenching, but it turned out the only thing you can do for a seizing back is rest, at first, and then stretch. The stretching will hurt, by the way, and it's not a good hurt, it's a nasty one, like a bad tooth. It's only after you keep at it for a week or so that you start to push through it.

This time it hurt like a bitch for three solid days. It was probably made worse by the fact that I insisted on going to this flea market anyway. Mom and I were excited to see it listed since it was hosted by the church that runs one of my favorite thrift stores ever. The church is one of those nouveau nationwide chain churches, like a T.G.I. Fridays. Mom didn't try to talk me out of going so off we went, her driving and me maneuvering myself in and out of the car carefully.

When we got to the church's big parking lot I was aware of seeming odd, though no one seemed to notice. I had to hold my head still and to the right, so it looked like

I was looking over my shoulder at something. There were lots of tables set up and I wanted to look at things but every time I forgot I couldn't turn my head to the left and turned it anyway I went "Yah!" I was able to buy a yellow and a green picture frame from Ikea in that light cheap wood they use. They were sold to me by a girl who was raising money for her youth group to travel to Uganda, where they will help build wells for water or something. I also found, on a blanket on the pavement, a fabulous red leather bag. It's one of those old-fashioned carry-on cases for air travel. Mom had come over to show me the book of vegetarian Italian cooking she found, and I don't think she was all that impressed with the bag, maybe because she remembers them. I think it's great looking. I bought it for a dollar from a man and woman who both had long messy grey hair.

I went home with Mom after the sale and watched TV on her couch. I could hardly move and I didn't want to be in my apartment alone. I ended up spending three days and nights there, lying awkwardly on my side and watching about 16 hours of TV a day because I was in too much pain to sleep past six a.m. Since I work from home as a freelance writer I didn't have anyone to make excuses to, but I still hated not getting anything done all week.

My low activity level made the delivery of the weekly paper feel much more momentous than usual. I anticipated it for two days and it came a day late, which is not unusual—you get the feeling they're publishing that thing as a hobby, and sometimes I wonder if we're the only people who read it. But you know, I love community newspapers. All this talk about the Internet replacing newspapers, it's been more or less true for the big city and national papers. Most people don't get their news that way anymore. But I don't think anything has come along to replace what community newspapers offer: a bit of neighborhood gossip in the police log and real estate and classified sections. In the crime log of our local paper I once read that a goofy guy I grew up with, a kid from my sister's class, had gotten arrested for public intoxication outside the bar up the street from me. He's a dullard but he's kind of mean too, so I found this mildly amusing. Then when I looked at the date and time I realized I'd been there that night with a friend, and I'd had a pretend-pleasant argument with the guy. (He insisted it was a Thomspon Twins song in the movie *Ferris Bueller's Day Off*, the part where they go to the museum. It's not, it's a Smiths song, covered by some other group. After a few minutes of conversation he said, and I quote, "Since you're a girl and girls never admit they're wrong I'm just gonna let it go." To which I said, "Well, I'm not wrong, and I'll never let it go." My friend and I cackled our heads off. She said I should have it put on my tombstone: *Here lies Katie. She was right about the Smiths.*) According to the paper, to my great pleasure, he got picked up by the cops that very night, about 20 minutes after I watched him stagger out into the early evening. I mean, the New York Times is never gonna chuckle with you over something like that.

But once I start waxing pretentious about the newspaper business I know it's time to get out of the house. We found a flea market listed in the classifieds—"Hundreds of Unique Items!"—and that became the thing I dreamed about in front of Judge Joe Brown for the next two days.

Unfortunately it wasn't great. These people's idea of flea market wares were manufactured tschotschkes done in that fake country Americana look. No thanks. I did buy one small green glass bud vase for a dollar. It shined up nicely when I ran it under the tap and rinsed the dust out. Now it sits on the deep windowsill of my bathroom, along with my collection of jade plants and other small vases and old glass medicine bottles. Pretty.

•　　•　　•

Grey Gardens Returns! These folks host this huge neighborhood-wide sale every year. The first time we went I bought some awesome stuff: a small wooden cabinet with sliding doors where I keep my records, a set of rubber stamps with wooden handles and an alphabet of nubby letters to slide onto their rows, and an orange wooden dining chair with a green seat. It was a great haul, and Mom and I were excited to check it out again.

It did not disappoint. First of all, some background. My friend Mandy recently emailed me a link to a craft blog with instructions on turning a small vintage suitcase into a tool kit. The blogger made hers to store her paper-making supplies, and Mandy thought it looked like the kind of thing I'd use in the zine workshops I do for kids. Too right, Mandy! I'll be doing the workshop at a library later this summer, so I've been on the lookout for some kind of case to carry my stamps, gluesticks, scissors, and other zine-making supplies. I could hardly believe my luck when I saw it: the exact same suitcase as the one on the blog, only mine is blue and the blogger lady's is green. It's perfect, though I had to buy a set of three suitcases—one inside the other like nesting dolls— and I don't know if I'll have a use for the others.

At another house I found an old wooden box with a hinged top. Mom pointed to it, knowing it was a Katie item, whatever it was. I asked the woman sitting there if she knew, and she called over to her husband. He laughed and said "Oh, it's an old Rolodex—a proto-Blackberry." Har har. It may indeed have been used for business cards but it looks and functions like the drawer of a library's card catalog, and I had to have it. I am something of a hobbyist librarian these days because I have taken over the job of librarian for our garden club. They have a decent collection of books on gardening and arranging that they store in the closet at the church where we meet and they needed someone to organize them and oversee borrowing. I jumped at the chance, dork that I am. I like books, for one thing, and I enjoy organizing certain kinds of information. But beyond that I have a deep, almost painful love for tools that have been replaced by more efficient tools but are still useful. I believe in outfitting every endeavor, a la Max Fischer in the movie *Rushmore*. If you're going to do something, do it wearing a uniform and with a name badge and toting the accoutrements around in a handsome carrying case—that's what I say.

A good part of the excitement about my amateur librarianship is bound up in my desire to create and move into some obsolete work space, where typewriters are snapping away and everything is clearly marked by the appropriate rubber stamp, then filed away in a heavy drawer. In this dream I wear pencil skirts and floral-print blouses and keep my eyeglasses on a chain around my neck. My look is attractive but not sexualized, utilitarian and pretty, and my attitude is friendly but brisk. I want to crawl inside this fantasy and live there, and anyone who wants to play along and act civilized and decent can join me. Everybody else, stay out.

At a house up the street I bought a sweet-smelling cigar box from an eccentric older woman with messy dark hair. From some other people I got a blue tin with the word TEA on it in white. These people appeared to be a married couple in their late thirties, very smiley but laid-back, like everyone else in this neighborhood. It seems like it would be an okay place to live. There was a third person, a guy around their age who was sitting on the small cement porch smoking a cigarette. He looked kind of pensive and thin so I had him pegged as the AA brother-in-law. Everybody's got one! He was sexy and I think I caught him noticing me.

Incidentally, the next morning I was in my apartment puttering around, studying my purchases and catching up on emails I needed to write, when a bird got into the building. Mom stopped by, and when I answered the door she was standing there all electrified and went "There's a bird in here!" I leaned out into the hall and sure enough, the poor animal was flapping around the high part of the ceiling over the stairway to the second floor. It was an elegant grey catbird with round black button eyes. I knew we had to get it out before it hurt itself or then we'd be stuck with a dead bird. It's always unnerving in a strange way when a wild animal gets indoors, isn't it? Even men get freaked out by it. It flew downstairs and sat on the metal bar that opens the back door. I wanted to let it out but I was afraid it would fly at my face. Something flying inside, the concept of *flying inside*, is weird. None of my neighbors were around, or else they were hiding inside their apartments. Mom and I took turns letting out little yelps and opening the front and back doors until suddenly the bird just flew straight out the back door as I held it open, confident and perfect, and lighted on a low branch of our great big horse chestnut tree and sat there like nothing had ever gone wrong.

IF YOU'VE EVER WRITTEN A BOOK YOU KNOW, AS I do now, that you finish it in fits and starts, not all at once but over a period of time. In a sense you don't finish it at all, you just stop fiddling with it eventually. But I like to say that I finished this book at the Anchor Archive in Halifax, Nova Scotia, where I spent two weeks as a resident zine writer, because I more or less did.

Let me tell you about it.

I arrived in this small city by the ocean late on a Sunday afternoon and dragged my suitcase to the cheerful, ramshackle, red-painted wood house in a careworn neighborhood north of the city's center. The house used to be the home of a couple of women who wanted to start a zine library, so they started it there, and the whole thing grew so much they eventually had to move out. My bedroom was a shed beside the house that's fitted with a comfy bed, a couple of lamps, and some shelves. And a mirror, which I rarely looked in.

At first being a resident there felt solitary, in a mostly nice way. It fulfilled—partially, anyway—some of my old fantasies of getting locked in a public building overnight. After the last member of the collective had come to check email, or screen-print t-shirts, or drop off greens from the farmer who hooks them up at the market, I could sit by myself on the busted couch in the library room and read all the zines, comics, and novels I found there, if I wanted to, and that is in fact what I tried to do at first.

But then fun and interesting things started happening. One afternoon I went to the beach with a couple of women from the collective and we went swimming in the ocean. I didn't have a bathing suit so I pulled off my dress and swam in my underwear, even though the beach was packed with people. Normally I'd feel too shy to do this but being away from home on my own gave me that fuck-it feeling I always crave and rarely achieve. I got battered by much bigger waves than I'm used to and afterward we went out for hot, oily-crispy fish and chips.

I also lived through Hurricane Earl, which hit Nova Scotia with some force and knocked out the power for a weekend, not just in our little neighborhood but in most of the province. That night, hours after the rain had stopped, I sat on the front step and read by daylight for as long as I could, and when it was about to get completely dark I lit the handful of taper candles I'd trash-picked a few days earlier and put them in a mug. I huddled up on my favorite couch and found I was able to read the novel I'd found in the library (*A Girl Like Sugar*) by my candle mug, and even though it was spooky I loved the adventure of it. The bad loneliness I'd felt that morning as the storm howled and rattled at the windows had leaked away, and at bedtime I felt as safe and content as I'd ever felt, snug inside my shed bed. I wasn't even scared at bedtime, when normally I'd have to shut up the Centre's main house and walk alone across the silent lawn to enter my little hut in the dark. That night it seemed like the whole world was dark, which made my own small spot of darkness seem not real, if you know what I mean. I even let my feet hang off the end of the bed: totally fearless. Before I fell asleep I shut my eyes and pretended that outside my hut was a zombie apocalypse, that I was the last person on earth, and it felt delicious.

A few of the people who drifted in and out of the house were uptight punk snobs, which was tiresome, but the good people were unusually good. One night I shared a dinner with a sweet woman from the screen-printing collective and her boyfriend and their friends, who'd caught a pile of mackerel in the harbor and cooked it up on the grill. On another night I helped make a beautiful huge dinner with a guy I'd met when he walked into the zine library and we had a great conversation about nostalgia and possessions and nesting. He and I walked through the neighborhood together, stopping first at an Indian grocery store for rice, spices, and chana masala, then at the community garden for tomatoes and peppers, and ended up at his house. In ones and twos his friends came by and shared the meal with us. One of them brought a hookah that we smoked fruity tobacco from, and when she said goodbye later she hugged me so hard my back cracked. Later that night his housemate dressed me up in a blue wig and eyeliner and we lay back on her bed and watched Boney M. dance St. Vitus-ly in Youtube videos projected onto the wall.

One day toward the end of my first week there a woman named Sarah came crashing into the library where I was holding court on the couch. She wanted to meet the resident writer so she could do an interview for her radio show. When I took her to the shed to get my zines to show her she told me she'd done the residency "back when this didn't have a door." She and I hung out for days after that, playing Scrabble and buying weird stuff at the Salvation Army. We became, I think, friends for real. She came with me to the art supply store, and helped me tape my event fliers to telephone poles, and showed me shortcuts through lumpy, weedy lots. One time we were walking down the sidewalk at night and I fell down for no reason at all. Didn't trip over anything, just fell. Isn't it stupid when that happens? She invited me to join her on a different interview, so together we took the ferry across the harbor to a town called Dartmouth to visit the Smiley Face Museum, an unbelievable few rooms crammed with a million tiny trinkets, toys, dolls, and doodads covered in those iconic yellow smileys. I watched as she prowled around the room, poking at things on shelves and talking to the woman who'd opened the place, which was an addition built onto her house, as a museum. It was an odd and touching visit.

And meanwhile—lazily, reluctantly, distractedly—I was writing. Sitting in a small office on the second floor, ignoring some of the knocks at the front door, I finished the fourth issue of the zine and started making the zines into a book. In the closets and cubbyholes of the Centre I found dozens of plastic sheets of Letraset, which are transfers of gorgeous inky black alphabets in different fonts that you rub off onto paper with a pen or other hard object. They're old things, from the sixties and seventies I think. I admired them all week, and over coffee one morning I had the idea to make an elephant shape out of them — an alphabet elephant — so I did, and I put it on the flyers that advertised my yard sale.

Yep. It was my turn. Roberts Street residents are required to plan an event where they will present the work they did there. As far as I'm concerned readings can be dreary—at least the way I do them, I get so nervous—so I wanted to have a party of some kind. I sat down with a different Sarah, one of the center's founders, and talked about possibilities. She suggested a yard sale, but how could I do that, really? I'd have to solicit donations from the community and I didn't know anyone. But after a few more days there I felt like I did. I told everyone I saw about it and over the next week, in the library, it grew—a small mountain of sweaters, books, antique cameras, pots and pans and hats. On the Saturday before I went home I endeavored to sell it all. How weird. All these years, all this thinking and writing about yard sales, and I'd never had one of my own.

That morning No-Door Sarah showed up and she and I sat on folding chairs on the lawn like two old men. I made up prices on the spot and ended the day with about 55 bucks (Canadian). (When you say "bucks" to Canadians, by the way, they won't know what you mean at first and might think you said the word books, which is confusing.) I sold a slide projector and an old wooden school desk and some other junk, and collected the money in a hard plastic rabbit bank I'd bought at the Salvation Army with Sarah. Then the rain that had been toying with us all morning came for real and chased us inside. We sat in the dim library and I read a section of my zine to a few people while the rain pattered down, and when it was over I felt relieved and happy.

The Physics of See-Saws
Yard Sale Season No. 4

YARD SALE SEASON 2009 STARTED OFF ON A GOOD-slash-bad foot this afternoon with the rummage sale at St. Martin's, a Lutheran church where Mom and I know a couple of congregants who we're always vaguely worried about running into. We haven't yet.

The good part is, I love St. Martin's rummage sale. It's always crammed with kooky stuff, like the beautiful Olympia typewriter I got for two bucks last year, and the people I see shopping there are my dudes, you know? The sweet, eccentric, talking-half-to-yourself-half-to-anyone-standing-nearby types. The kind of people who take the bus, who carry old tote bags with book festival emblems with them on the bus, the kind of people who could probably talk to anyone about just about anything but prefer to keep to themselves most of the time. The kind of people no one else in the world ever wants to be around for some reason. People like me.

My mom does not belong to this group, not really. Sometimes that fact is more evident than others, and today was one of those times. That was the bad part. She looked unnecessarily freaked out by the large number of people in the old church hall, all kicking at the shoes on the floor in an attempt to try them on, or picking through the contents of ancient cardboard boxes; squeezing past each other between the cafeteria tables piled with clothing and stiff, musty sewing notions and unidentifiable hunks of plastic that someone doing the organizing thought looked like office supplies, murmuring "Excuse me" and "Oh, of course" and joking "Don't look at me!" when someone accidentally sent something clattering loudly to the linoleum floor. I was the one who said "Don't look at me," actually, but a sweet-faced old man with shaking hands smiled and said, "That's what my wife used to say." I mean, these are nice people. But Mom looked so aggrieved and jumpy the whole time I had to avoid her.

Then again, I was up until 3 a.m. talking on the phone last night and I have my period, and I think I'm falling in love with the person I was talking to, so I feel a little fragile today, a little tender, in one of those moods where every pretty thing I see or think of hurts my feelings. So it could have been me.

Anyway, wanna know what I bought? I found a long flowered sundress with pockets and a wide belt. I tried it on at home and it is a winner. The fabric is covered in purply blue flowers on a black background and it has a drapey, slippery heft to it, it's not flimsy or skimpy at all. It hits at the ankles but I think I'll lop a good foot off the bottom of it, maybe more. I'd like it to go above my knees, maybe. I just have to be careful not to cut into the pockets. I should probably shorten it not all at once but bit by bit to make sure I don't mess it up.

I also bought two clear plastic bookends with, like, holders in the front that I think will be perfect for displaying my zines at the Philly Zine Fest. I bought a small brown paper sack of buttons for the person I think I'm falling in love with, because he likes to sew and I know he'll find a use for these. Even better, they're man buttons, tan-colored ones and ones with textures like the kind that would be on a professor's corduroy jacket.

I also got a few books—one "real" one, an anthology of short stories by North American women, and two oddball ones. At this sale they put the books on card tables up on the stage. It's a church hall/auditorium sort of room. At the foot of the stage are all the shoes, lined up neatly at first but eventually more or less in a pile. One of the jokey books I found is a small saddle-stitched book called Symbols of the Church, Together With Saints and Their Emblems. This is excellent. I like church lore, I especially like the saints and their stories, and I like heraldry and symbolism in any form. There's a glossary too. Ablutions! Affusion! Even the modern-day, post-Vatican II church comes with an awful lot of documentation—like a car, the glove compartment crammed full of papers you need to keep and sort of understand just to keep it running. I have to say I like this. I like the idea that there's a university's worth of stuff you need to learn in order to belong to a religion. I've never minded a little studying.

The other book is this thing from 1959 called Music For Young Americans, and it's the annotated teacher's edition. There's very little about this book that is American per se. I think it's just from an era of talking about everything in an oddly nationalistic way, and I find that interesting. The cartoon drawings of children and animals are sweet, and the back of the book gives detailed instructions on what the songs are good for and even how the children should be directed to sing them. "Use this song to awaken the children's interest in the rhythms which they hear in the home, on the street, and in the air," says one, and "Be sure that the children sing this piece reverently, in thanks to God."

I like the thing about singing reverently, it's just an invitation to faking it. It reminds me of when I was a kid, studying for my first confession. One day my mom and I were going over the questions and answers we kids had to memorize, and I said in a very serious and hushed way, "The important thing is, when you confess your sins you have to sound really sorry." My mom couldn't help it, her face exploded into a smile and she chuckled and was like, "Well, I think you're supposed to be sorry, not just sound like it."

At this rummage sale, underneath a stack of paperbacks, I also found the front and back covers of a scrap book—the tall hardback kind, probably from the fifties to judge by the gold cursive writing on the front, with ribbons to tie them together with your pages in the middle. You can probably picture the kind of book I mean. I resolved to commemorate something soon and create a scrap book; something I have never done. You just put pages and then tie it all together, right? I mean, I could do this. It seems like as good a way to spend a summer as any.

• • •

Well, it's a week later and I'm still dopey in love. The object of my affection—his name is Joe—lives an hour or so's drive away, and he came to stay with me on Thursday and Friday. Actually, he arrived in the middle of the night on Wednesday because the place where he was supposed to stay that night, on "some bummy couch," was the site of a party that already had too many other people bumming couches and he would have had to sleep on the floor, and we'd so wanted to see each other again that he got in his car and drove through the city to get here instead, through one of Philadelphia's roughest neighborhoods. Picture a zombie movie, picture the Apocalypse. That's what it looks like there. But I forgot that was the way he'd have to come and I told him, "Yes, come whenever you want, and if I fall asleep just call me and I'll wake up and come down and let you in." So he did. He woke me out of such a deep sleep that I thought it was a joke when the voice on the phone said he was outside. What do you mean outside? Outside of my house? In the dark, in the grass? Yes. I padded downstairs, squinting in the hall light, and found him there, waiting for me.

The next day he wanted to sit in the sun so we got a beach towel and he brought down his nice laptop filled with all this music I've never heard or even heard of and we sat and listened to it. One thing about spending time with a guy who's ten years younger than you are, he's probably gonna know a lot of bands you're unfamiliar with. (Yes, Joe is ten years younger than I am. Neither of us can feel the age difference, though I'm sure you can see it in our faces. The only time it really comes up is in conversations about music, like when I'd never heard of Peter Bjorn and John and he couldn't remember the Ginuwine song "Pony.") I lay down flat on my back at one point and stared up through the horse chestnut tree, which was trying to dizzy me with its lazy moving leaves that let the blue sky and bright light show through. The taller the tree, the further away from you those leaves are, the slower they seem to move. I remembered seeing a big camera obscura set up at an arboretum one time. It was a stuffy rounded structure sitting in the middle of a field, with a heavy curtain door that blocked out all the light. One tiny hole let in an image of the outdoors, splashing all those trees across the wall of the hut like they'd been painted there, only upside down and backwards but sharply defined, and tiny. And the magic part was that it wasn't a photo or a drawing. It moved. I stood in front of the wall and watched the leaves bouncing slowly, slowly like the trees were underwater when they were so far away.

That weekend Joe and I made zines in the Office. The Office is a new game of our devising, for which we both dressed in the secondhand "business" clothes we've collected over the years. The point of the Office was to make zines, to wear clothes we like, *and* to make fun of the stupid office jobs we've both had, but whenever either of us told a friend about our plan we were embarrassed by their universal assumption that it was a sex thing. It isn't! It's a zine thing. It did end up being a little sexy, though. At his request I zipped myself into one of my pencil skirts and wore a silk blouse tucked into it, a pretty collared one in a kind of pearl shade, and I wore my favorite navy blue pumps with clip-on blue and silver flowers. He brought along some posters he made and hung them in the Office, one of which is a somewhat complicated bar graph depicting our phone conversations, with his mood on one axis and the time spent talking to me on the other. He wore a yellow tie, and since I'd seen him last he'd shaved his beard but left a sleazy mustache that looked so good. We talked about zines, but we didn't get much work done.

At the end of the week was the sale at St. Peter's, which is another favorite, one that Mom and I look forward to every year now that we've become old hands at this sort of thing. They hold the first part of it on Thursday evenings and my mom is never up for going out after dinner, so we go the next morning. That's when they have their "bag sale:" three dollars a bag or two bags for five. You can shove anything into one of these brown paper grocery bags and believe me, I do.

One thing I found was one of the *Better Homes & Gardens* cookbooks I like to cut pages out of and make into envelopes. These are plentiful at rummage and library sales. This one is called the "**MEAT COOK BOOK**," just like that, in all caps. I love the pictures in these because they are so gross and garish. The food tends to look terrible—things like Jell-o molds with horrible sliced hotdogs in them, or mayonnaise-thick salads, but it's not just that. The photography is outdated too, so the combined effect is awesomely gross and nearly science fiction-grade weird. I tear pages out and cut and fold them up into envelopes, then sell them at zine fests in sets of four, tied together with twine. The zine kids love repurposed stationery like this, and I try to be sensitive in general to not bring the ones with meat on them to zine events since so many punks are vegetarian or vegan, but this one is so awesomely terrible I had to get it.

The other books I got were Kate Chopin's *The Awakening*, a feminist classic supposedly but a book I've never read, and a quirky little picture book from Japan called *Finding My Way*. I don't think it's meant to be quirky, just to be cute. The story is about a humanoid creature that goes trundling through fields and forests on its way home but gets lost on the way, and this idea combined with the disjointed, short sentences of odd English is almost haunting, but not quite. Mostly it's a novelty.

I also found a soft black shawl thing that I will wear in the winter, and a hot pink silk blouse with a lot of flouncy stuff up near the neck. Back at home I tried it on and it doesn't fit close on my body but instead falls straight, creating a very late-seventies, early-eighties *Nine to Five* secretary meets Fashion Plates vibe. Do you remember

Fashion Plates? Maybe you're younger than I am, or older. When I was little there was this plastic toy that let kids make fashion "drawings" as though they were designers. They were plastic with raised images you could combine however you wanted—cowgirl boots, mini skirt, peasant blouse, yeah!—and then make rubbings of them. It was fun. In any case, this blouse will be excellent for the next round of Office.

On our way out a tall skinny woman tried to get Mom and me to buy the bigger stuff near the front door. She seemed nervous. "Do you need a piano?" she asked, a bit frantic, as though this could be an impulse buy, or something we'd been meaning to pick up but just kept forgetting. It turned out she was stressing because she was going to have to clean and put away all the tons of leftover stuff from the sale in time for a meeting taking place in the hall that afternoon. Bummer.

·   ·   ·

There's not a lot to say about the New Life Flea Market so I'll just tell you about the few nice moments. New Life is a church, and a few blocks from here is the huge thrift store they run, which is one of my favorite places in the world. The flea market they held in the church's large parking lot. I found six records for four dollars, including some great ones, stuff by Isaac Hayes, Blondie, a couple of Rolling Stones albums, Elvis Costello's first one (*My Aim is True*), and Stevie Wonder. They were sold to me by a couple around my age, a tall sweet caucasian guy with his equally smiley Asian girlfriend. I also found, on a card table in the blazing sun, salt and pepper shakers that look like tombstones that read here lies salt and here lies pepper.

Mom went off on her own while I was fondling the tombstones. When I found her she was holding a coleus, its bright green leaves veined in fuchsia. She told me that a teenage boy, who she pointed to while she said this—and waved when he looked—had grown all the plants he was selling from seed. Later she flirted with a dude who sold her a glass vase. He was trying to get everybody who walked by his table to buy this silly decorative hobby horse, this big painted thing hung awkwardly from one of the metal poles of his tent, right behind his head. My mom was touching the vase and he said to us very brightly, almost maniacally, "Ya wanna horse?!" I thought maybe he was your garden variety flea market kook but my mom seemed to vibe him more accurately and understood that he was joking, flirting. She teased him back: "I don't need that horse!" and it was funny to watch her talk to a man like that, just an easy kind of flirtation, because she hasn't done that much in recent years.

In the classifieds that week we were surprised to see that Old Man Bread had rolled around again. Where does the time go? This sale kind of sucks though, I must say. We look forward to it and go every year but mostly just for old times' sake, since it's one of the mainstays of the season. At this point we feel obliged to our own tradition: I pretend to get excited about it and also pretend to chastise my mother for being less excited about it, and then we get there and I never find anything good. My mom takes the the sleeping old man we once saw sitting by the door and the day-old bread they sell there as proof that the sale is pathetic, but I try to stay positive—and unlike her I see no problem with the bread and once bought a perfectly good bag of bagels there.

However, this year I was in bad shape. I didn't sleep last night, never even went to bed until around six a.m. Something bad happened, something to do with Internet stalking and my new love, and instead of calling to ask him about it I sat in the armchair in my living room all night, chain-smoking in the dark like a serial killer. I keep trying to quit but at times like this it's impossible. At the sale I concentrated on trying not to cry, and bought a ceramic jack-o'-lantern candle holder to put on top of the bookcase in my living room. My thinking was that even though it's not the season for Halloween its shape and color would be cheerful and nice next to a round, cornflower blue clay vase I have up there.

Joe and I set things right after Old Man Bread but not before we had a long, miserable conversation about it. I learned that I had misunderstood the Internet thing and let my imagination go wild, and when we were done talking it through, everything seemed okay again and I wasn't sure why I'd ever gotten so upset. "I've been so unguarded with you!" I sobbed at one point. I was exhausted and useless for the rest of the day.

Needless to say I was still up for a little rummaging the next day, though, which is lucky because that morning there were two sales right within walking distance of my apartment. Mom stopped by my place to visit with Trixie before we made our way over to the first stop, Joan's Church, so called because it is the church where mom's neighbor Joan goes. They do their sale twice a year and it's usually in two rooms in the church hall but this time it was outside, on a handful of small tables at the back of their parking lot. This church has several small buildings on its lovely grounds. They look straight out of an English village. I poked around at the sort of dinky offerings on the tables and found a floral plastic bangle bracelet that I liked and some shoeboxes full of cassette tapes of classical music. The woman who'd donated them helped me choose a handful. "How about Bach? He's got something I think, if he sticks with it he could go places." I also found a National Geographic book on Federal Lands for my sister, who likes that sort of thing.

Joan's Church isn't that important though, not in light of the other thing that was taking place today. A tag sale at the convent! Man were Mom and I excited for this. Seeing inside the convent of the nuns I knew growing up has become a fetish of mine. Some of the women who lived there, who taught me in school, were probably decent enough people.

Some of them were so mean, it was like they drank poison every day just to stay evil. The building itself is small and beautiful, with only a few simple details to embellish it, like the small cathedral windows and whitewashed stucco. Some sick part of me wants to move in there and make it my home; the other part still wants to deface it with angry graffiti.

I put on my new bracelet like it could give me good luck or protection and we looped back to the convent from Joan's Church, crossing the street through impatient traffic to get there. On the lawn of the convent were two cafeteria tables with folded linens and glassware arranged with psychotic tidiness. No one lives in the convent anymore, incidentally. The nuns who'd taught me in school left when I was in the fifth grade, and some other nuns came and lived there for a while, and then no one did. They just use the rooms for meetings and stuff now, I think.

I fingered some eyelet lace cafe curtains and wondered: Are we allowed inside? A lady I'd known growing up was there and I smiled and chatted with her and I wondered: Are we allowed inside? Before I realized it Mom was boldly striding up the walk toward the front door. "Oh yes, there are other things laid out in the dining room, I almost forgot" the lady in charge called out to Mom, and I hustled to join her. What a coup. There we were, creepiness of creepinesses, standing in the convent where Sister Martha and Sister John used to live.

And it wasn't creepy at all. It was pretty, exceptionally clean like every speck of dust had been removed, but not bare. The front rooms had a light-colored, tight-knit wall-to-wall carpet, glass curio cabinets with glaze and gleamed up at me like a penny on the bottom of the pool. It should read: The front rooms had a light-colored, tight-knit wall-to-wall carpet, glass curio cabinets with doohickeys in them, and a polished wood dining table and chairs. The rust-colored tiled floor of the entryway was thick with glaze and gleamed up at me like a penny on the bottom of the pool. I peered through the dining room into the kitchen, which was industrial but not that big, and reveled in the feelings of fascination, longing, mild discomfort, and extreme coziness that rolled confusingly through me. The truth is I felt so safe in that house I could have curled up on the floor and gone to sleep. I stopped having anything to do with church the minute I came of age, which had the funny effect of making me think the place had disappeared when my childhood did. Going into that convent—which was indeed abandoned and empty—felt like stepping inside my own memory.

I bought that eyelet curtain, which turned out not to fit my kitchen window, and an amber-colored beveled drinking glass that I chose because it looked particularly nun-ish and like a chalice to me, but which I have since seen in thrift stores more than once.

· · ·

Is everyone bored of me gushing about this guy I'm dating? I would be. Don't worry, I'll give it a rest this week. Let me just tell you about Grey Gardens, the neighborhood-wide sale that's become one of our yearly favorites.

This year it was hot and people seemed less into it, but we still had fun. At one tidy little house I bought a metal toast rack for one dollar from a sweet elderly couple— two women. I didn't know what it was but Mom did. She said it was an English thing, to prop up your slices of toast in there before eating them. Do English people like to eat their toast cold? If so, why? These ladies had the nicest sale we found that day, with all their pretty, simple things thoughtfully displayed, not lots of junky Beanie Babies and what have you. Let me say, a heap of Beanie Babies and old children's clothing does not a yard sale make. Not one that want to go to, anyway. And I've got a better use in mind for this thing than toast. A zine rack! It's the perfect size for displaying small books. It's good too because it's small and hardly weighs anything and since I don't drive I've always got to carry all my zine fair supplies in my backpack, on some train or bus.

At someone else's house I got that Modest Mouse album *Good News For People Who Love Bad News* on CD for a dollar and at a third place, which mostly had jewelry I didn't care for spread out on tables, I found a resin owl figure cut in half. Each half has a strong magnet to draw the two halves together and the woman who sold it to me explained that you're supposed to put one half on the inside of your window and the other on the outside. Neat! When I got home later I discovered I can't do this because the windows are double-glazed, but oh well. It was 25 cents, and maybe I'll be able to use it in the next place I live. I never used to think about moving away, but since I met Joe I've started thinking about future things. Having an adventure like that with him, starting over someplace new, has begun to seem like something that might happen someday.

As Mom and I strolled through the winding treeless streets of this suburban neighborhood we saw the occasional interesting thing, like a big rocking chair with an elaborate bentwood design, but nothing that grabbed us. And it was getting hot and humid on those bare streets so we made our way back to the car. I'd had pretty good luck but I didn't feel ready to end the day's rummaging, so we looked at the classified section again, which we had rumpled on the floor of the car. There was something advertised as a "book sale" that had started on Thursday and today was supposed to be the bag sale, with everything reduced in price. These terms are not usually used to describe a yard sale at a person's home, so we were intrigued. Was it something shady, like a dealer pretending to be a regular yard sale and using the classified section to advertise? Mom and I have encountered that before. Truthfully we didn't much care one way or the other, but we did agree that we wouldn't appreciate living next to someone who was running a store out of her home on the low.

We drove slowly on small back roads with the windows down till we found the place, a beautiful, if cluttered and run-down, Victorian house. It was darkish inside, but I think Victorian houses might often look like that, with the dark wood of everything, and the heavy-looking staircases, and the ornate but not-so-large windows. The front rooms, one of which had a stained glass window in bright colors, were filled with books, most of them old, in cardboard boxes on the floor. There are days when I'd be in the mood to look through all of them carefully, but this was not one of those days. We poked a bit though. I was excited to see a book of Keats' love letters to Fanny Brawne. I've been interested in this love story since that Jane Campion movie Bright Star came out last year. It was lovely, if a little overwrought, symbolism-wise. I'd made this guy D. take me to see it. D. is a British guy I dated for a few icky months at the end of last year, and even though we didn't make a good connection and he wasn't especially forthcoming or open or nice to me, I kept banging my head against it, trying to make it work. I was infatuated with the idea of him, this English guy who'd quit his job—his career—as a banker in London and went to live in different parts of Asia for five years, and now was here, getting an MFA and writing a novel. It serves me right that he turned out to be a jerk. Why did I think I could objectify someone that way? The publication date in the Keats book is written in Roman numerals, and whenever I figure those out I have to put the shock paddles to my dying grade school memories. Eventually I worked it out to be the year 1878. Pretty old!

But it was in another box on the floor that I made the best find of the day: a small black leather journal from 1949, which someone faithfully kept nearly every day in pencil. "Oh Katie, that has your name all over it," my mom said. Indeed. At first it looked like the only thing the person recorded was the weather, but then I was able to see it was household stuff too, almost like a job, and I'm thinking that's what it is, like the records from a boardinghouse maybe. In a different box Mom found three more books like it from the years 1945, 1939, and 1932. "Katie, I think this is quite a find, we're gonna have to get these," she said, and I agreed. The lady, a fair-haired and skinned person who was relatively young but looked like maybe she'd had a stroke with one half of her face slack, charged us one dollar apiece for the books. Note to self: I owe Mom seven bucks.

I'VE GOT THE MODEST MOUSE ALBUM ON NOW. I
know a handful of these songs and the ones I don't know I'm
liking a lot. Fun, totally worth a buck, and I like it when Isaac
Brock screams like Frank Black. I now think that the journals
belonged to a carpenter, since he seems to be talking about
finishing projects of one kind or another, including a door,
and that would explain his interest in the weather, since that
has a big effect on that kind of work. Now I know I said I
wouldn't talk about the guy I'm dating, and I won't, but let
me say I've had a funny weepy feeling today and yesterday.
He was here with me last week, and we had a picnic in
the playground behind the creek that runs behind the train
station. It was a beautiful June day, clear and cool, rich blue
sky—almost an autumn sky—with dazzling spots of sunshine
coming through the tree branches all around us. I wanted
him to push me on the swings, and he did, but I got off soon
because it was making my stomach feel tender, not exactly
nauseous but fragile and full, like with a hangover. Then
we sat on the see-saw, and I can't remember the last time
I played on one of those. The physics of it has always kind
of perplexed me—do both people have to weigh exactly the
same amount, or what?—but Joe felt more comfortable with
the concept and jumped up onto the middle of it and surfed
the thing, letting it fall fast enough to be exciting but gently
enough that I wouldn't fall backward. I couldn't help it, I let
out a little shriek every time I bounced down on the tire
stuck in the ground. It always went down just a bit lower than
I thought it would go.

Two people, one was a guy and I couldn't tell about
the other one, went past us on the path on their bikes, all
tricked out in that tight-fitting biking gear. The one guy smiled
at me, and it was a smile with a fair amount of information in
it. He looked the way you do when you're enjoying yourself in
a certain way and it pleases you to see someone else having
the same kind of good time. I haven't gotten a lot of looks like

that in my life. More often than not I've been by myself, and I very much like being alone, but somehow it doesn't seem to bring out much in the way of goodwill in other people.

Joe and I sat on the beach towel that Pat next door gave me. She turned 90 this year. When she gave it to me she said with a laugh: "My beach days are behind me." After a pause she added, "You could use it to sit outside." She'd seen me and Joe out there, and I could tell she thought the time I've been spending with him seemed nice. I guess he and I have the blessing of the whole neighborhood. The ground was hard underneath us but the towel felt soft and clean, like home. I had a lot of feeling in me, sitting there with him. It's that difficult time of year again, the anniversary of my dad's death, but this year was a little different because lately I've felt crushed by happiness, too. I had that feeling where your chest feels full, and it makes you a little short of breath.

Before Joe and I sat in the playground we looked in the creek and saw a lot of fish. There were some pretty sunfish with their sweet flat colorful bodies and it made me think of summers in Maine, fishing off the dock at the lake where our cabin was. We called the cabin a camp. It was this one-room hunters' shack that my dad and uncle built an addition onto—two bedrooms, one for my parents and one for me and Liz. Sunfish were all I ever caught, and we always threw them back. I can remember how their hard, flexible bodies felt in my hand, and the flapping feeling of their wet paintbrush tails, the way their gills would cut you if you didn't slide your hand down their bodies the right way, and the hollow cracking sound it made when you popped the hook out of their stiff mouths.

When we were done with our little picnic and it was time for Joe to go home I waited with him on the train platform and watched him get on, watched him walk down the center aisle, looking for a seat. There's something especially sad and almost scary about that, when you can still see the person you've just said goodbye to but they can't see you. It feels final, like your separation has made you gone for real.

And sure enough I cried hard the whole walk home from the station, openly and publicly, but no one was around to see. It's hard for me to say goodbye to people in a way it didn't used to be—even that stupid guy D., who I never even really liked. I kept waiting to hear from him even though he hurt me with his stinginess and standoffishness, kept putting off telling him I didn't want to date him anymore because it crushed me to think of there being one more person in this world I wouldn't see again, one more goodbye.

I woke up the next day still sad. I rode the train from Philadelphia to Joe's town in central Jersey for a craft fair, where we've been selling things every Friday in the month of June. I felt uncomfortably, unreasonably angry the whole way there. A woman bumped into me hard on the train platform, I mean she bounced off of me, and she didn't turn to apologize or even acknowledge it. Rude, but I fantasized about calling her names, and I knew my reaction was too strong.

As the train got closer to town I realized I felt afraid to see Joe. Ah, so I wasn't angry, I was sad. I didn't want to cry when we were supposed to be having fun but I didn't think I'd be able to stop myself so I felt nervous about seeing him at all. When we pulled into the station my chest and throat ached like they always do when I'm stopped up with tears like that. I wanted him with me but I couldn't go to him so instead I lugged my bags across the street to the beautiful colonial cemetery that's there, at the top of a steep slate staircase. I sent him a text message telling him where I was and I couldn't say more but it was okay because, to my surprise and relief, he remembered why I was sad, and he came and sat next to me on the bench without saying anything and just held me while I cried into his neck. I hate crying, even when I'm by myself. I always panic, like once I start I'll never be able to stop.

We went to the craft show but I felt like I was moving underwater, too quiet and subdued to talk to anybody, but it didn't matter because most of the people were just jerks preoccupied with their little kids anyway. What a mess, I was too scared to go use the bathroom at the coffee shop by myself so he came with me and waited while I went in. That night we lay on the big air mattress in the guest room, where I sleep when I come to visit, and he stroked my back and sang me a song in a soft voice. He really did. No one's ever done that for me before.

I woke up the next morning on the air mattress alone—at Joe's parents' house, where he lives, we're not allowed to sleep together. I went to go wake him up, pushed open the door to his room with a shhhhh as it rubbed against the thick carpet. We'd been looking forward to going to this yard sale Joe had seen advertised by a sign on the side of the road ("Huge Yard Sale This Saturday"), and I didn't want to miss it. After kissing and coffee we got permission to take his dad's car, since his died a few weeks ago and he hasn't yet figured out how he's going to afford to replace it. You know how summertime always feels like the sixties or seventies, like you could be a hippie with your messy hair and bare feet? His dad's car is a van with a dream-catcher hanging from the mirror, and that made me feel like a hippie too.

We turned off the main road onto the smaller one where the sale was supposed to be and got out. It was only 10:30 but it was already brutally hot in the sun. There was the yard sale, pretty big as promised, and the garage door was open too—always a good sign. Joe started chuckling and saying Well, hello there or something and it turned out that this man had been his high school drama teacher. He shook the man's hand and reminded him who he was, using his full name. He sounded like such a grown-up man doing that, it touched me.

The guy Joe knew walked around and shouted out prices and deals like a carnival barker. I found a bunch of identical "Brat Pack" DVD sets still inside their plastic packaging, which seemed shady and I thought the guy was sleazy but I couldn't tell if Joe thought so too so I didn't say anything. I got one of those DVDs. You better believe I did. It has *The Breakfast Club* and *Sixteen Candles* on it. Not *Pretty in Pink* though, to my disappointment— that's my favorite of that "genre." The whole thing was a nice distraction, but back at Joe's house my body felt heavy again and we had to hide upstairs in his room because I'd started crying again. We lay down on the bed and put on *The Breakfast Club* and watched it till I calmed down and with his dad downstairs we had sweet, slow, almost silent sex in his childhood bedroom. Afterward I sipped at a cup of water while we talked, and Joe said we could hide upstairs forever if I wanted. Then we played about 47 games of Uno, and eventually I settled onto the solid ground inside myself. Crying forever isn't actually possible, I guess. You always start to feel good again, eventually, even though you know the time to be sad will come back.

· · ·

And now here it is, two weeks later: the Fourth of July. Fourth of July, why are you always so good? All spring and summer we've been calling our weekends the "Best Weekend Ever," but this one really was. With his parents' help Joe bought a car to replace the one that died and he loves it, and I love being in it with him. We can listen to music with the windows down and just drive around my neighborhood, I don't even care where we're going, even if it's just to the stupid bagel place with the awkward parking lot.

But before he came to see me Joe had to have a yard sale of his own.

He grew up next to his grandparents and they've both died within the last six months, and now his parents are going to sell that house, most likely to a developer who will level it and build a big ugly "mansion." Watching the house get knocked down by machines is almost too sad to think about, but Joe lives with his parents next door so whenever it does happen, they'll see it. They have a houseful of old-people stuff to deal with first though, and Joe thought having a yard sale might be kind of fun.

It wasn't, I don't think. They made about seven bucks, and he ended up keeping a heavy old medical encyclopedia for himself. He called afterward to tell me, first of all, that a horrible man who vaguely knew Joe's grandpop had stopped by and was forcing him to be an audience to his racist rants about the "new" people in the neighborhood until Joe was able to slink away, and also that there were kitchen things of his grandmother's I could have if I wanted. I told him sure, thank you, I'll take them, just get in the car and come see me now. When he got here I helped him bring in paper bags heavy with his grandmother's things: a big platter that might be a cake dish, heavy ceramic mugs, and a small stack of delicate, mismatched plates. My favorite ones are white with blue roosters and swirly designs painted on them: breakfast dishes.

And you know, there's so much more I could tell you just about this one dumb summer day. I want to tell you how later that evening we walked to my mom's house where we cooked out and ate a quiet dinner on the patio with her and my sister, who offered us this special beer she likes. I want to tell you that we went to see the fireworks at the high school and how magical I find fireworks to be, how they're never boring and I don't care if bugs are biting me or the grass is sticky. I want to tell you what it feels like to be in Joe's car with him, rolling through the neighborhood on a hot summer evening that's slowly getting darker, a warm glow coming from people's windows like fairy lights, going to see the fireworks like I used to do with my parents when I was a kid, but it's hard because I'm afraid it will only come out cheesy. I think I'll just trust that you know how I felt that night and leave it at that.

BE OUR "BEST FRIEND FOREVER"

Do you love what Microcosm publishes?
Do you want us to publish more great stuff?
Would you like to receive each new title as
it's published?

If you answer "yes!" then you should subscribe
to our BFF program. BFF subscribers help
pay for printing new books, zines, and more.
They also ensure that we can continue to
print great material each month! Every time
we publish something new we'll send it to
your door!

Subscriptions are based on a sliding scale
of $10-30 per month. Please give what you
can afford so that we can be sure to send
out more stuff each month. Include your
t-shirt size and month/date of birthday for
a possible surprise!

microcosmpublishing.com/bff

Minimum subscription period is 6 months. Subscription begins the month after
it is purchased. To receive more than 6 months, add multiple orders to your
quantity.

Microcosm Publishing
636 SE 11th Ave. Portland, OR 97214
www.microcosmpublishing.com